'Utulei,
My Tongan Home

Patricia Ledyard

As a child wading in the cold surf on the beach of her native San Francisco, Patricia Ledyard dreamed of the lands that lay on the other side of the great Pacific ocean. During World War II, as a public relations officer with he United States Women's Army Corps, her dream began to come true when she was assigned to Australia, New Guinea and the Philippines. After the war, she returned to her native California, but wanting a more leisurely civilian view of the 'other side', she went to New Zealand where, while studying anthropology, she became interested in the island Kingdom of Tonga. Deciding to spend a year there, she got a job as headmistress of a girls' secondary school in Vava'u, the northern Tongan group. Marriage with Farquhar Matheson, a Scots doctor who was working in the Vava'u hospital, raising their two children and becoming an integral part of the community changed her mind about the length of her stay which has now stretched to 44 years and which, she hopes will last as long as she lives.

By the same author
    FRIENDLY ISLES, A TALE OF TONGA
    THE TONGAN PAST

'UTULEI,
My Tongan Home

by

PATRICIA LEDYARD

Vava'u Press, *Tonga*

Published by Vava'u Press Limited
Haveluloto village, Tongatapu
P. O. Box 427, Nuku'alofa, Tonga, South Pacific

© Patricia Ledyard, 1974, 1993
First published in Great Britain 1974
Paperback edition, Tonga 1987
Reprinted, Tonga 1993

ISBN 0 908717 07 5

First printed in Great Britain by
Bristol Typesetting Co. Ltd.
Paperback edition printed in Singapore by
Chong Moh Offset Printers

CONTENTS

1	A Thank you	9
2	My Four	12
3	Did You Adopt Her Legally?	27
4	The Queen comes to Tea	29
5	As the Twig is Bent . . .	43
6	At Home in 'Utulei	46
7	A Brief Note on Missionaries	63
8	The Doctor and the Young Men	66
9	Ve'emumuni	75
10	A Picnic and Talafaiva	77
11	The Story-telling Weaver	83
12	'Utulei Beach School	85
13	The Turtle	93
14	The Judge's Story	96
15	On Preconceived Notions	104
16	The Haunted House	106
17	Misconceptions, Tongan and *Papalangi*	111
18	The Hurricane	113
19	Hili Afa	127
20	Tapa de Coty	130
21	Charlie's Present	142
22	Queen Salote Tupou	146
23	The End of Handsome Men in Tonga	153
24	The Cave	156
25	A Case History	168
26	A Tongan Triangle	172
27	Doctor and Friend	180
28	A Circular Story	183
29	Changes	191

ILLUSTRATIONS

facing page

Important people: Tu'ifua, Farquhar, Tupou and Tami	64
The house at the point	64
Tu'ifua	65
Farquhar with Tami	65
Tupou and Tami on the beach (E. Kenney)	65
Back to the house (E. Kenney)	80
The Mathesons	80
Sunset view of Vava'u Harbour from Neiafu (S. Dean Ritterbush)	81
The house	81
At a village feast	128
Tupou and Tami dancing at a village celebration	128
In the wake of the hurricane: the wrecked school-house	129
'Utulei village with our house in the foreground	129
Farquhar and Felemi in the wreckage of our bedroom	144
Mataisi with Semisi in what remained of his house	144
The author	145
Tami, Betty Buck and Tupou in Boston	145

Except where acknowledged to another photographer all the above illustrations were supplied by the author.

Map	10
Plan of the house	49
The house at 'Utulei, illustration by Jean Tufui 1987	cover

PREFACE

'UTULEI 1987

"HAS TONGA changed much? How is development affecting the country? Don't you get tired of living in such a remote spot?"

Those are the questions which in endless variations, visitors ask me nowdays and they are the ones I shall attempt to answer here in this preface to the new edition of *'Utulei, My Tongan Home*.

First, I must point out that it is now nearly forty years since I came to live in these islands. In those years great changes have come to the world, to Tonga, to my home in 'Utulei and to myself.

When first I came to this country, it seemed to the white people here that there were great differences between themselves and the Tongans and so there were. Skin colour was the most obvious, but the least important. Vastly more significant were the differences in life-style, in general knowledge of the world and in the overall aims of the two groups. Yet, those differences had not always existed. Indeed, when Captain Cook and his men came, the lives of common people in England and in Tonga were much the same for both lived on the land.

What differences there were, were those inherent in the two countries—one having a temperate climate, the other a tropical climate, one being rich in minerals, the other poor, one being close to a continent on which many varying cultures had developed, the other lying in the great ocean in which there were scattered island groups which all had the same basic culture. As the son of a poor day labourer, Cook, himself, would have had no difficulty in relating to ordinary Tongans whose work was raising food and whose pleasure was eating it.

You may well ask what happened in the roughly 200 years between Cook and the other early explorers and 1949 when I arrived in Tonga that had caused white men to feel so different from brown ones and so much superior to them. Put briefly, it was the Industrial Revolution.

More earth-shaking than the bitterest war, the Industrial Revolution was, of course, not a single event, but a whole series of inventions. The steam-engine, the spinning-jenny, the power-loom, new processes of manufacturing steel—were only a few of the things that altered for all time the lives of ordinary men. Some of those inventions had, of course, been made even before Cook started to explore the Pacific, but they had not then come into general use. However, had Cook lived out his normal lifespan and spent his old age in his native land, he would have found the world a very different place from what it had been when he was a boy. As most of the initial inventions of the Revolution were made in England, it is perhaps, not surprising that the English soon came to feel that they were more clever than any other members of the human race.

In England and in the other countries that followed her into an industrial way of life, there were suddenly great oversupplies of the commodities of everyday life. Things have a vicious way of making their possessors long for more things. It soon became obvious that, if they could sell their surplus, they could manufacture and buy ever new things.

Sellers need buyers and it occurred to some brilliant man—or group of men, that if the backward peoples of the world (by whom they meant those who lived in lands not yet touched by the Industrial Revolution—most of whom, as it happened, had skins of a darker hue than the industrialists) could be made to want their products, they would have the money for which they now found an increasing need. And so it followed that England and the other great powers sought colonies. Most of them were gained through war with rivals, but sometimes they were merely taken from the natives who were powerless before the white men's more sophisticated weapons. If the English felt an occasional twinge of conscience at what they were doing to other peoples, they were able to quieten it by telling themselves that they were helping others to rise, although it was inconceivable and undesirable to them that their darker skinned brothers could ever reach their own superior level. Their beliefs were sanctioned by the pious churchmen of the day who quoted from Joshua about the "hewers of wood and the drawers of water" which allowed them to feel thoroughly justified not only in exploiting native peoples, but also, when it suited their purposes, in enslaving them.

For a long time—over two centuries in many cases, the colonies dutifully fulfilled their function of supplying the mother countries with raw materials and buying back the goods manufactured from them. A relatively small part of the manufactured goods was books. Was it from them that the coloured people of the world first learned to dream of political independence or did they come to it by some other means? At any rate, the dream was born and persisted and grew until countless places in Africa and the Pacific and the rest of the world broke away from the great powers and emerged as independent countries. Faced with loosing their submissive markets, the mother countries were in a quandry. War and simple seizure had come into such popular disfavour that they no longer seemed a possible way to secure new markets. It was then that the idea of development came into being. If the emerging countries could be helped to a higher stage of material development than they had known as colonies, their people would want ever more things and would provide a never-ending market for manufactured products. It is true that the moneys poured into emerging countries reach staggering amounts, but they represent only a small part of what the major powers expect to get back on their investment.

There is, of course, an alternate explanation of development which springs from the attractive if probably fallacious notion that the path of humanity is always upward. It claims that the consciences of the powers awoke, that they pitied their less fortunate brethren and belatedly felt that notwithstanding differences in skin colours, they were worthy of having all the good things which the Industrial Revolution had provided for white men.

That explanation is, naturally, gratifying to *papalangis*, many of whom chose to believe it.

Be that as it may, just as Captain Cook's own world was changing as he explored the Pacific so the world of the industrialists was changing as the idea of development swept through their countries. A whole complex of new inventions has again shaken the world, hastened its pace and widened its horizons. To it we give the name, the Electronic Revolution. Unfortunately it has come to the world before the world's emerging countries, or for that matter, before the industrial ones, have been able to digest thoroughly the Industrial Revolution.

So the world at large. Now what of Tonga? In 1970, it gained its independence. Although it had never been a British colony it had been bound to England by a Treaty of Friendship which in the eyes of most

Tongans was merely a gentlemen's agreement of mutual aid and trust, but to the world at large made the country into a protectorate. By 1970 the British Empire had disappeared and in its place had come The Commonwealth of Nations which independent Tonga obligingly joined. Although the dominant influence remains English, nowdays Tonga has dealings with many other nations all over the world, most of which do their bit toward development.

In Nuku'alofa, the capital, which lies 170 miles south of Vava'u, it is comparatively easy to pinpoint changes as they come, but in the little village of 'Utulei, it is difficult to say just when men's lives and men's thoughts began to alter, but undeniably they have changed.

For one thing, although Tonga is, to all its loyal citizens, the centre of the world, horizons have expanded and it is no longer the whole world.

When first I came to 'Utulei there were people here, old ones as well as young, who had never been as far away from home as Nuku'alofa. I remember a British civil servant who had worked in the Holy Land who came and talked about it to the village men. At the conclusion of his speech one old minister thanked him profusely, saying that he had never known that the places mentioned in the Bible were real. He had imagined them "made up" to point some moral of Christianity.

Nowdays when all the people listen to radio such ignorant innocence is no longer possible. Not only do our people know about the world beyond Tonga, but many of them have seen it for themselves. There is not one of the thirty households of our village which does not have some family member who has travelled overseas. In many cases they have been in foreign places for part of their education. In others they have worked in distant lands.

If it is true that church and children and food are still the main preoccupation of islanders, it is equally true that changes have taken place in them all. The new Wesleyan church in the village is made of concrete blocks. It has its own generator to supply light for night meetings as well as give power for the video machine that now provides so much of the village's evening entertainment.

The Tongan families which in the old days often counted as many twenty children have gone out of style and today's newly-weds say four is enough. What is more, they are as knowledgeable about birth control as any of the young overseas.

Money, a Tongan friend told me in my early days here, was

something *papalangis* had. Nowdays it is something everyone has or at least wants. Certainly everyone needs it for the corned beef which has long been a staple of Tongan diet and used to cost 20 cents a can now sells for over $2.00; cement has risen from $2.00 per sack to $10.00, and the thongs that once sold for 75 cents a pair now cost six or seven dollars. I could extend the list endlessly, but to do so would be futile. It is simply that inflation which makes life increasingly difficult in the outer world has come to these islands. Those Tongans who work at jobs (and they are an ever increasing number) get monthly salaries that once would have seemed vast fortunes, but nowdays can scarcely be stretched to buy what has come to be regarded as the bare essentials.

Young men returning from stints overseas with their pockets stuffed with money and their heads awhirl with the wonders of the outer world have broken down the centuries' old dominance of the aged. After all, who wants to listen to grandfather tell how to burn out the centres of a log to make a canoe when he has seen fibreglass boats powered by engines capable of whizzing the long miles to the end of the harbour in a matter of minutes? And who is now content to lie in the warm darkness of tropic nights listening to grandmother tell what the village was like when she was a girl, when he can go off and watch the village video or stay at home and switch the radio on to the world?

The amazing thing about Tonga is not how skillfully it has adapted to the modern world, but how much of old Tonga still exists. The pace of life has quickened lately, but Tongans still find time for laughter and for friendliness and sharing remains for them the only true way of life.

When I was first in Tonga only the present King and the head of the Wesleyan church, had university degrees. Now there are hundreds of BA's and MA's and a respectable number of Ph.D.'s and MD's. Many of these educated young Tongans come home to work. Others find that, in order to use their knowledge to the greatest extent, they must remain overseas. But whether they live here or far away, they are still true Tongans and, having enjoyed the widened horizons of a university education, are anxious to share it with others. Overseas remittances from relatives pour into Tonga constantly. A high percentage of that money is for school fees; for, education has, in modern Tonga, become a primary goal.

And so the world and Tonga has changed and my own little bit of it has changed, too. As I have written, our home at the point, when we first bought it was a shell which we at once set about transforming into the home we wanted. Now it seems that change is as much a part of this house as it is of the world and of Tonga; for it is still going on.

Since first I wrote this book, the house became too small for our growing library so we had a separate large airy room built in the back to house all our books.

Sometime after Farquhar died a visiting New Zealand carpenter crawled under the house and announced that the wooden piles on which it stood would collapse shortly as termites had been busily gnawing away at them. The collapse of the piles would have tumbled my home into ruins so, in a major operations, I had the house transformed from a wooden one into a concrete one. While that was going on, I had a second storey added on to part of the house and so gained two extra bedrooms.

As I write this our old school room is changing into an orchid room and my bedroom is getting a new wing that will house my painting materials.

And so from the world, from Tonga, from 'Utulei, from my house, I come to myself and I, too, have changed. From a young bride, I have become an old widow. My white hair shows no traces of the red it once had, although Tu'ifua assures me the temper associated with red hair still shows.

Naturally, I hope that in some small ways I have changed for the better, but it would be more seemly to leave that to my friends to comment on. Basically, just as much of the old Tonga comes through in the Tonga of today, I think much of the old Pat still flourishes in me.

Certainly I still find every new book, every new plant, every new friend, every new day exciting and never have I felt more at one with the village people than I did on this New Year's Day when they poured over the fence at dawn as they've done every year I've been here and gathered on the lawn below the verandah to sing for me the New Year's songs which are at once praise to God and thanks for all his blessings.

Let those who will mourn for the good old days. With the people of 'Utulei, I look forward to the good new days to come.

'Utulei 1987

To
My JWLs

CHAPTER ONE

A THANK YOU

I HAVE lived forever here in the little village of 'Utulei on Vava'u harbour in the Kingdom of Tonga. Here I have been old and young, known sorrow and joy, failure and success and all the other stuff of living. Here I have learned to love—and what is just as important, to consider those I cannot love. I have laughed and shared delight with my neighbours. I have wept and been comforted by them. Here I have read books, listened to music and made plants grow and here I have, myself, grown and sent down roots that hold me firmly to this island so that I have become as much a part of it as are any of my brown-skinned neighbours whose remote ancestors were blown to these shores by some fortunate wind in the distant days that belong not to time, but to myth.

And yet, it seems only yesterday that first I sailed down the long island-lined way that leads to the quiet inner harbour, only yesterday that I discovered the grassy paths that wander by my neighbours' gardens into the wild bush land; only yesterday that I met the people whose lives have been woven into mine.

Forever, and yesterday. It is a strange double time-scheme that attaches itself to my Tongan years, but I think the best periods in all lives are measured so. As a matter of chronological fact, it is now twenty years since I came to Tonga. The ship that carried me away from my native California to New Zealand and the one that brought me a year later to Vava'u were properly named and registered. I myself had a passport and tickets and all the usual paraphernalia of a proper traveller. Yet my trip—as surely as that of the first Tongans, was a drift voyage. I floated here on the restless tide of youth, full of that melancholy wanderlust that is a search for a way of life and for the people with whom one wants

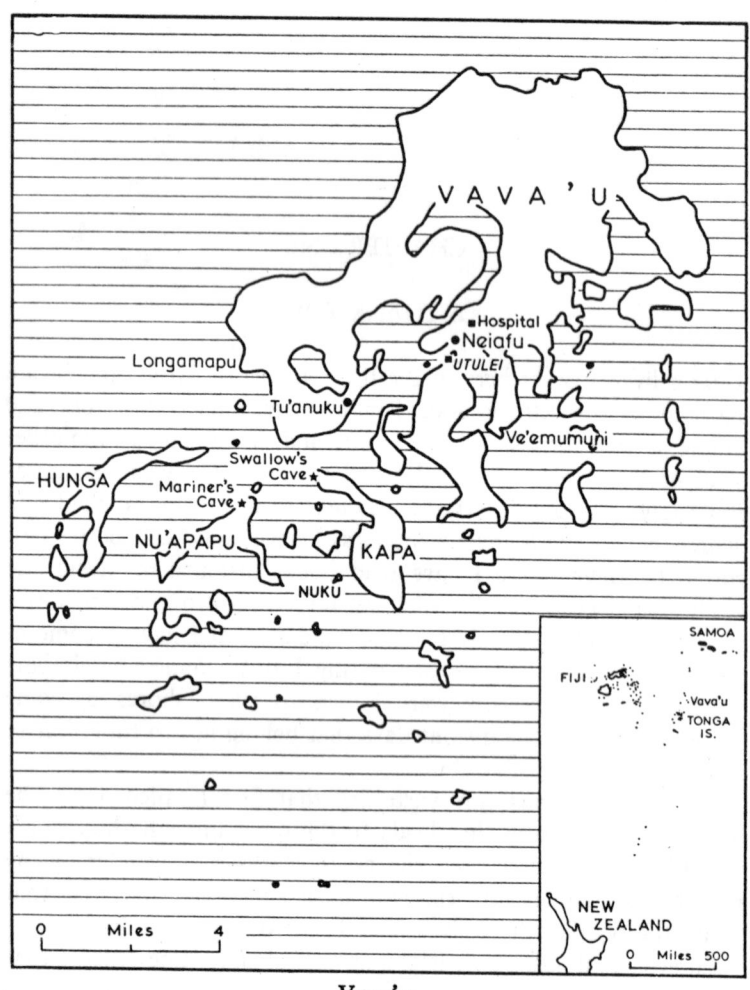

Vava'u

to live it. Like those old time Tongans, I was fortunate. They found here everything they wanted. So did I.

When I came, I was alone. I brought little with me—only a bag with a few clothes, a case of books, a year's contract for a job as headmistress of the Wesleyan girl's college in Neiafu and an eagerness to commence on the period of time I then referred to as " my Tongan year".

A THANK YOU

Now, already, that year has stretched into twenty and I hope I shall be here still when, for me, all years end. I have not adopted my Tongan neighbours' way of life any more than they have adopted mine, but, perhaps, living side by side all these years has made life richer for both them and me. Certainly I have learned much. The first Tongan word I learned was *"malo"* which means "Thank you" and the first thing I learned about the Tongan people was that they find occasion to say it far more often than the most polite *papalangi*, or white person ever does. They do not limit the word, as we are apt to do, to a conventional acknowledgement of presents or acceptable social behaviour, but use it to express their constant gratitude for every good thing that God offers to man—for each new day with the works and pleasures that it brings, for each rest-filled night, for the miracle of birth and the equal miracle of death.

It is because I have learned from my neighbours that gratitude is the proper attitude toward life that I have written this book. I want it to say "Thank you, Tonga". Thank you for your islands that lie in beauty on the sea. And thank you for your people who—although they have all the faults of people everywhere, have been given more than the common allotment of kindness, tolerance and merriness—and, especially, thank you for the villagers of 'Utulei with whom I have shared the days that have grown into my Tongan years. Above all, thank you for the four who, here in Vava'u became my people—for Tu'ifua and Farquhar, for Tami and Tupou. And a final Thank you, Tonga, for having made me feel at home in your islands—and in this world.

CHAPTER TWO

MY FOUR

MY FEELING for Tonga was love—not at first sight, but even earlier. The year before I came here, I spent in New Zealand, studying anthroplogy at the University of Otago with the famous Polynesian authority, Dr. H. D. Skinner and it was in his library, in some musty old books with cracked leather bindings, that I first discovered these islands. Reading through the long grey Dunedin days, I soon fell completely under the spell of Tonga which Captain Clerke, who sailed with Cook, described as " one compleat garden ".

Because, in pre-European days, Tongans had no written language, an exploration of their history runs quickly into myth. Gods and goddesses mingle freely with people, an unbelievably large and active force of devils complicates life, men and maidens change themselves at will into animals or stroll casually in and out of this world through the gate that leads to Pulotu, the Polynesian Paradise. To read the history of Tonga, to go back so quickly to the shadowy time of myth, is to leave our chaotic modern society and to find a whole new world that offers all the the beauty, all the freshness, and all the simplicity of the early Greek world.

The god, Maui, began everything here. It was he, the great fisherman who, on a sunny day, baited his hook, cast his line into the sea and caught, one after another, the islands of Tonga. When he had pulled them all up into this world, he looked at them and congratulated himself on a good day's fishing.

At the time I first read of Tonga, in Dr. Skinner's library, scholars believed that these islands remained just as they were on Maui's fishing day—bright, green and untouched until the ninth century of our era. They thought that about that time various groups of people in Asia—forced by overcrowded conditions, by hunger, war, or harsh rulers—or perhaps only by man's eternal curiosity, began to leave their homeland. By the slow process of island-hopping, speeded often by unintentional drift voyages, they came down into the Pacific. In time, they spread out through all the vast ocean area that is known today as the Polynesian triangle which stretches from New Zealand, the home of the Maoris, clear across the Pacific to Hawaii, from there down to lonely Easter Island and so back again to New Zealand.

In the last few years, the Pacific has been overrun with scientists of all sorts, foremost among them, anthropologists. With their spades they have dug further and further into the Tongan soil and into the Tongan past. Today they still believe that man came to these islands from Asia, but now, mainly as a result of the development of the carbon dating process, they have pushed the probable date of his arrival back as far as 800 B.C.

Old memories preserve records of battles between the Tongans and their Polynesian kinsmen and neighbours, the Samoans. There were, too, minglings with the Melanesian Fijians and with other peoples even more distant, but, in spite of such contacts, the Tongan way of life seems to have been basically undisturbed through many centuries. Only with the coming of Europeans was it to be radically changed.

Although the Dutchmen, Jan Schouten and Jacob Lemaire had sighted the northernmost islands of Niuatoputapu and Niua Fo'ou in 1616, they did not actually land, but contented themselves with trading with the natives who came to their ship in canoes. Not until almost thirty years later, in 1643 did Abel Tasman, another Dutchman, become the first European to set foot on Tongan soil. He was favourably impressed with the natives and reported that "all was peace and friendship".

In spite of his good report, it was 124 years before another European came to Tonga. In 1767, Captain Wallis in the 'Dolphin' paid a one-day visit to Niuatoputapu. He was the first representative of England, the country to which Tonga was to become so closely allied. A far more important Englishman—the most famous of all Pacific explorers, Captain James Cook, made his first trip to Tonga in 1773 and, in 1774, during the course of the same voyage, visited it again. He returned in 1777 on his last trip to the Pacific and explored and charted Tongatapu and many of the islands in the Ha'apai group. Hearing of the beautiful and fertile northern islands of Vava'u, he wanted to see them, but the chief, Finau whom he regarded as his great friend, told him it would be impossible as there was no adequate landing. Considering that Vava'u has one of the largest and safest harbours in the Pacific, one can only conclude that the false Finau was the first of a long line of Vava'u people to question the desirability of tourists.

Captain Cook went away without having seen the most beautiful of all Tongan places, but Finau could not for long keep Vava'u from Europeans. On 4th March 1781 the Spaniard, Maurelle, anchored in the group and came ashore to be entertained by Pau, the Tu'itonga, (or spiritual head of the country). By the eighteenth century, Vava'u was well known and, like all the rest of Tonga, was visited by successive waves of French, Portuguese, English, Spanish, Dutch, Germans and Americans who came searching for gold, whales, spices, souls to save, the fabled continent of Atlantis and a thousand other things—not the least of which was sheer adventure.

An inability to understand one another's language and customs resulted in some misunderstandings and a few fatalities for both Tongans and the early explorers; but, staying for only a few hours or, at most, a few months, those first comers did not change in any appreciable way the life which the natives had led for centuries. They did, however, open the way for change. Before the eighteenth century was over, the first convicts escaped from the penal colony in Port Jackson and the first missionaries had both arrived. Between them they broke the old pattern of life and Tongans were forced to begin the process which is still going on, of trying to fit their age-old customs into the rapidly-changing modern world.

As time went on, the hours I spent reading of Tonga became my most important ones, but soon I realised that reading was not enough. I had to see this place for myself. A regular tourist cruise was out of the question. I could not afford it and, furthermore, I knew that a few hours or even a few days in Tonga would not be enough for me. Remembering from my reading that the Wesleyan church was in control of education, I wrote off to the head of the Mission asking him if, by any chance, he had a teaching job open. By return mail, I was offered the place of Headmistress of Siuilikutapu Girls' College in Neiafu, Vava'u. The salary was minimal, but I did not care. The job would take me to Tonga and give me a chance to spend a year there.

I sailed from Auckland on the old *Matua* in January—which is to say, in the middle of the hurricane season. The second day out, we ran into a storm which tossed and battered us until after we had left Fiji when it dwindled out into drippy leaden skies and sudden squalls. The morning we were due into Nuku'alofa, I was up on deck early, but it was a grey world that greeted me—grey seas, grey sky, a monotone of grey in which the horizon had disappeared. In vain, I looked for land. Finally I asked a passing officer if I were looking in the right direction.

"Yes," he said, and, pointing to what looked like a dirty pencil smudge against the universal grey, "That's it."

"That," I repeated questioningly, "That thin line?"

He laughed. "I suppose it's not much like your dreams of tropic islands."

"Not much," I admitted, but nevertheless, I felt a growing excitement.

My excitement was shared by a vast number of people of whose existence I had—until that moment been totally unaware. When I had come up, I had picked my way through a strange cargo we had taken on board in Fiji—pigs, chickens, baskets, rolls of mats, and miscellaneous mummy-shaped packages bound up with brown *tapa* cloth. As we neared Tonga, the packages began to stir, mats unrolled, *tapa* covers were thrown back and from them emerged my first group of Tongans.

Although Polynesians are among the world's great navigators, they are also the worst of sailors—and habitually when travelling as deck-passengers lie, as these Tongans had done, like the dead. Resurrection came with magic speed as the *Matua* carried us ever closer to land. Before my eyes, young women sat up, pulled the drab wrinkled dresses in which they had slept over their heads and replaced them with bright printed gowns, old men sat in groups singing hymns of rejoicing and thanks for the journey safely ending, merry-eyed children ran mischievously about from one group of elders to another and babies were fed and wrapped into smiling packages of contentment.

Although I could understand none of their chatter, I could not mistake their eager anticipation which burst out into delighted shouts when, for a minute, the clouds lifted and revealed a flat shining green land. I made out a few houses strung along the water front and off to the right, set back in spacious gardens, the dazzling white Royal Palace—that famous old story-book structure built in the ornate style best described as Victorian gingerbread. A glimpse—that was all I had before a sheet of rain, falling like a stage curtain, shut out the view and sent me scurrying down to the cabin for my raincoat.

By the time I came up on deck again, we had docked. The Tongan passengers crowded thick against the railings, but, as I approached, a kindly old man beckoned to me and squeezed me in beside him. Below us, quite undaunted by the rain which continued to fall, was a great crowd of men and women and children. Their upturned brown faces were smiling as they waved and called out greetings to the passengers around me. It was an infectious sort of gaiety. I, too, lifted a hand and waved. Instantly a sea of hands waved back and a whole chorus of voices shouted, " *Malo e lelei, malo e folau!*"

In halting English, the old man beside me explained, " They say, 'Good day and thanks for sailing to here'."

Such friendliness rose with their greetings that I leaned even farther over the rail and waved again, but a heavy touch on my shoulder and a disapproving voice in my ear made me whirl around.

" You are the new teacher, I believe." The voice that spoke was Australian and cold.

" Yes, I am," I replied and felt a sudden panic as I looked into a pinched ferret-like white face.

" I am the Reverend Branard Christopher Pauson, president of the church in Tonga," the owner of the face was saying as he replaced a sombre black hat on his head. He paused for a moment to let the full effect of his name and title sink into my consciousness before adding, " My car is on the wharf. Come, please."

Obediently, I turned and followed him. As he went down the gangway and through the crowd on the wharf, the people drew aside, making a passage way for us. Respectful of him they obviously were, but I thought it an uneasy sort of respect; for, as he approached all their natural gaiety disappeared. Smiles left their faces. They fell silent. Once I stopped and while he went on a bit, the crowd closed about me. When I smiled at the people, they responded again, " *Malo e lelei, malo e folau*", and the warm feeling I had known on the ship returned. It was not destined to last long. In a minute, Mr. Pauson was back.

"I almost lost you in this crowd," he said, but from the note of accusation in his voice, I understood well enough that what he really meant was that I had lost him.

"Follow me closely." At the command, I trotted behind him, while the rain beat down on us with renewed fury.

I tried, as we drove away from the wharf, to see something of the town of Nuku'alofa, Tonga's capital city, but through the rain-splashed windows I could see little and Mr. Pauson was no guide. Indeed, the task of driving seemed to occupy him completely. He said not a word, nor could I, looking at his grim black-clad self think of anything to say to him. In a futile effort to escape a trickle of water that fell down between us from a hole in the roof, I sat leaning over toward the door wondering glumly if all missionaries were like my companion. By the time we had arrived at the Mission House, I was thoroughly damp and thoroughly dejected.

"The other members of the staff are waiting inside for you," Mr. Pauson said as we got out and walked up the path toward a big shabby house with a sagging veranda. I had a premonition which was very shortly justified, that they had come, not so much to greet me, as to inspect me. There were about a dozen men and women in the musty-smelling living room. They had been talking together in the harsh nasal tones of Australian cockneys, but at our approach, they stopped in mid-sentence and stared at me as if I were some strange sub-species of the human race.

"The American," I heard someone whisper in a disparaging tone just as Mr. Pauson began very properly to present me to each one in turn. Their names and their faces blurred in my mind until it seemed that they were all one—one wan smile, one look of disdain that made me wonder if I had forgotten to put on some essential item of clothing.

When the ordeal of introductions was over, we all sat down on the uncomfortable straight-backed chairs that lined the room and a frightened-looking little Tongan girl handed around cups of weak tea and plates of flaccid egg sandwiches. After a few comments on the state of the weather, Mr. Pauson bent toward me, coughed slightly and said, "We welcome you to this mission field and to the work we are doing for Jesus Christ."

B

I managed to mumble thanks, but I could not feel that his welcome was sincere. Nor did I feel that the other people in the room had any friendlier feelings although they had all begun to talk very spiritedly about Christian fellowship.

Encouraged by the topic, I asked whether there were not any Tongans on the mission staff.

"There are Tongan ministers in all the villages and Tongan stewards," someone said.

"Yes," I persisted, "but here on the staff?"

One of the wives, sitting beside me, said, "Oh, I see what you mean. You're wondering why none of them are here this morning. Well, you see, they don't eat with us."

"Oh," I said in so questioning a tone that she added quickly.

"We go to their feasts, of course. They like that, but they feel—well, uncomfortable in our houses. They don't know what to do."

I have learned over the years that it is a convenient article of missionary faith that—although Tongans rejoice in expressing their friendly feelings by offering feasts to white missionaries, it never occurs to them that the meals might be reciprocated. Already I sympathised with the Tongans. I, too, felt uncomfortable in the Mission House. Talk lapsed into what I was later to come to know as standard island small-talk—grumbles against the government and against house-girls, complaints about the difficulties of procuring European foodstuffs, grievances against the weather—all laced with a liberal supply of local gossip.

When I began to be uncomfortably aware that I should be contributing something to the conversation, I asked questions about Vava'u and the college there. I was surprised to discover that although Vava'u is only 170 miles north of Tongatapu, only a few of the missionaries had been there. Apparently they had been content to take Mr. Pauson's word that it was dull "outback" or "bush" country. From the reading I had done in New Zealand, I knew better. With, perhaps, more enthusiasm than politeness, I said, "I'll be glad to be there whatever it's like. I want to meet my teachers and get started at the college."

In a belated attempt to be friendly, Mr. Pauson turned toward me smiling faintly. "I've just remembered," he said, "your head teacher is here. Would you like to meet her?"

"I would, very much."

He tinkled a little bell that stood on a table beside him and the frightened looking girl who had served tea appeared.

"Go and get Tu'ifua," he said to her and, turning back to me, explained, "There's a teacher's conference on at the moment and all the church teachers from Vava'u are down for it. They're right out in back in some old school buildings, so she won't be a minute."

It was not long before there was a knock and the door was opened. The dark room and the drab missionaries with their pale faced, dowdy wives receded into the background as I looked up and saw a tall, handsome Tongan woman in her late twenties in the doorway. Garbed in a simple dress and long *vala* skirt made of some thin lavender cloth that made her brown skin glow golden, with a finely woven *ta'o vaka* (mat) tied neatly about her waist, she stood erect, proud, and perfectly still as if she were some chiefly woman from the distant Polynesian past surveying a group of commoners. Then, as if she suddenly remembered where she was, she lowered her head ever so slightly and, giving Mr. Pauson the polite form of address, asked " *Tangata eiki*, you sent for me?"

"Yes, here," and he pointed to the floor beside him as if he were calling a dog to heel.

If she was offended by his manner, she gave no sign that she was even aware of it. With regal grace, she moved across the room and stood in front of me. Mr. Pauson introduced us, gave Tu'ifua some senseless admonition about her duty to me and, to my great relief, moved away to talk to someone on the other side of the room.

The brown eyes that stared down at me were the largest and most beautiful I had ever seen in a mortal—and stare they did, relentlessly, as if they were trying to look into the depths of my being and discover what manner of person I was.

Embarrassed by such a scrutiny, I began to talk. "We shall be working together in Vava'u. I'll need lots of help from you. There are so many things about Tonga that I don't know!"

"I shall be glad to help you all I can," she said soberly. Then, looking across the room at Mr. Pauson she added, "It is my duty to do so."

I laughed. "I hope you'll find your duty pleasant."

In return, I got an unexpectedly friendly smile that made Tu'ifua's eyes sparkle with a deep glowing light.

Just as she was beginning to tell me about the college and about Vava'u, Mr. Pauson reappeared. "That will be all for now, Tu'ifua," he said in the flat tone of finality.

Both literally and figuratively, she looked down on him. I found myself being delighted because, although she treated him with the utmost politeness, there was yet a hint of arrogance which perfumed her relations with him as subtly as the sandal-wood oil which she wore scented the room.

"I shall see you next week when I return to Vava'u," she said to me and turning gravely bade the rest of the company goodnight and left the room.

"For a Tongan," Mr. Pauson said using what I was to come to recognise as a favourite missionary qualification, "She's very capable."

I felt a sudden urge to laugh, but, reflecting on the company I was in, refrained from doing so.

Lying in my bunk that night as the *Matua* rolled her way gently up to Vava'u, I tried to sort out my reactions to my first day in Tonga. They were extremely mixed. When I thought of Mr. Pauson and the slow hours spent in his stuffy parlour with the other members of the mission staff, I shuddered and wondered whether, with such colleagues, I could ever last out the year. Until that day I had never actually met a missionary. I had been prepared for them to be, in their religious views, narrow, but I had expected them to be also the most sincere of people, fired by a love of human-kind and desiring to call all men "brother". Mr Pauson and his staff had brought speedy disillusionment. It seemed that they knew nothing of love and that the last thing in the world they would do would be to consider a Tongan as a brother. Lest it seem that I arrived too quickly at my judgement, I feel compelled to say that twenty additional years of observing missionaries and listening to their talk has reinforced rather than altered my original opinion.

Had I had nothing but missionaries to think of it would have been a glum night indeed, but every now and then thoughts of those drab people were pushed aside by a bright memory of the deck passengers who talked and sang the night away and by the merry crowd that met the ship at the wharf.

And now and again, I once more saw, in my mind's eye, the tall serious Tu'ifua. I did not know then, of course, that in her I had encountered the first of my important people, but our brief talk had been long enough for me to realise I had met an unusual and complex person. I knew that working with her would be a challenge.

And so I drifted off to sleep. It seemed only a few minutes later that the stewardess was shaking me. " Get up," she said, " Or you'll be blaming me for missing the harbour."

Half-asleep, I mumbled a protest, but she was not to be gainsaid. She switched on the light above my head to make a return to sleep impossible and set a cup of steaming tea on the table beside my bed. I got up and dressed and by the time I had scorched my insides with the burning drink, I was wide awake.

When I got up on deck, we had already entered Vava'u harbour. Gone were the Pacific swells which had rocked us all night. Here the water was calm with only the white foam passage made by the *Matua* to ripple its surface. The rain clouds which had greyed Nuku'alofa had travelled north with us, but the morning had transformed them. As the sun rose, it burnished their undersides so that they hung above us—great reflectors casting a shining golden light over the ship and the sea and over the interlocked islands with their tangle of green bush lands.

Sometimes we passed so close to the shore that when we came to a place where the bush had been cleared to make way for a village, we could hear the shouts of the children who ran out of their thatched houses and raced along the beach waving at us. Sometimes the land opened giving glimpses of twisting waterways going off like side paths from the great sea road we were travelling. Then our way was blocked by a high-rising island. It seemed the ship would sail into the very centre of it, but suddenly there was a jangle of bells and we made a sharp turn, leading into the inner harbour.

Off to the right, there was a village whose houses straggled down a steep hill to a curved white beach. Behind the beach, just at the foot of the green hill, was a big old-fashioned white house with wide verandas. As I looked at it, a gentle rain began to fall, each drop a whirling round of light as bright as a Christmas ball.

" How beautiful it is! " I exclaimed aloud.

The ship's officer who had stopped by my side a minute before said, " That's the doctor's house—that big white place. He's a

Scotchman. He lives there all by himself. Says he likes it. I reckon he's mad."

"I'm going to work here for a year myself," I said.

The officer shrugged his shoulders. "You'll be sorry. It's a dead hole. You'll be sorry—unless you're mad too!"

He moved on and I stood staring at the house until it was lost behind the curve of the harbour. I turned then and saw from the opposite side of the ship, the scattered houses and the one street of stores of the big village of Neiafu which was my destination. We drew up to the wharf, the engines fell silent, and I heard my own name come creaking over the ship's loudspeaker. "Miss Ledyard, Miss Patricia Ledyard, passenger disembarking at Vava'u, report to Customs in the lounge."

There were two men talking together on the far side of the room as I entered the lounge. One of them, a big round Buddha-like Tongan who was dressed in a khaki *vala* and a uniform shirt liberally laced with gold braid, came toward me and smilingly introduced himself as the Customs man. When he had looked at my passport and collected my landing permit, he put on a very smart cap, tapped its shining black brim and said, "That's all except for the medical check."

He gathered his papers up and "This is Dr. Matheson," he said as his companion, a ruddy faced Scotchman with a shock of shining white hair, came up to us. "I'll leave you with him," and giving me a parting smile, he bustled off.

I held out my vaccination certificate and the doctor took it, gave it a cursory glance and handed it back to me. For a second his sky-blue eyes held mine, but when I asked, "Is that all?" he stirred and said in a deep voice, "Yes. You look healthy enough. This check is merely routine."

I was starting to leave when he spoke again. "I heard some time ago that you were coming. I hope you'll be happy here." There was a serious formality about his words, but a note of enthusiasm and a pleasant Scotch burr crept into his voice as he said, "It's a good country and the Tongans are fine people."

Impulsively, I said, "I saw your house as I was coming in. You have a beautiful place."

"Aye, it's beautiful." He stated the fact as one states the obvious. "After you get settled you must come and see me."

He told me then that he was going up to the hospital and asked if he could take me to my house at the college which was, he said, on his way.

That day, he was Dr. Matheson to me, but soon—along with the rest of the community, I was calling him simply "Toketa". When the college started I was responsible for over a hundred girls and I was most grateful when he offered to check them over at morning sick call. Most often when he had finished, we shared a cup of morning tea before he went on up to the hospital and I returned to classes. Before long he became Farquhar. In mid-May he became my husband.

Queen Salote used to say that rain brought good luck. I know that, as Farquhar and I walked down the gangway and onto the wharf on that first of all my Vava'u mornings, the golden rain which had followed the ship up the harbour, fell upon us. The luck it brought was very good. I had found the second of my important people. On my first two days in Tonga, I found the first two of my own people. I had to wait for the other two.

After Farquhar and I were married, the village of 'Utulei took us to its heart at once and it accepted Tu'ifua as a helpful older sister, but when a year had passed, the villagers began to murmur that we were something less than a household. A proper household has children and we had none. The women spoke openly of the lack and frequently suggested that it was high time that we "began to make a baby". By the time the second year had passed, the women no longer spoke to us of having a child of our own, but said with disarming frankness as they shrugged their shoulders, "Probably they're too old".

In the evenings we sat together on the front veranda and watched the village children playing amphibious games—now running along the beach, now plunging into the water. Against the setting sun, they made the gayest, most animated of silhouettes and their shouts and laughter rising up to us were a symphony of joy.

"What a wonderful place to be a child!" Farquhar would exclaim. " If ever I'm reincarnated, I want to be a Tongan."

But neither Farquhar nor I believed in reincarnation and in the third year, as we watched the sunset children, there was a touch of wistfulness in us that soon grew into a longing for a child of our own who could know the wonderful freedom of a Tongan childhood.

At the beginning of the fourth year, I had *"puke lelei"*—the good sickness. That euphemism for pregnancy is a significant indication of the way Tongans look on children. As soon as the villagers became aware of my condition which, in this land of little privacy, they did very soon, there was great rejoicing. " Now you won't be lonely", they told us. "Now you'll have someone to love you when you're old". Their rejoicing was accompanied by a vast amount of both curiosity and pride. After all, " 'Utulei had never before had a *papalangi* baby and they intended to make the most of it. One after another, the village women came by to conduct an endless seminar in pregnancy—its joys and its hazards. All such meetings ended in congratulations on the fact that my husband was a doctor.

" How lucky you are," they said, " he can do everything at home. You won't even have to go to the hospital."

Farquhar did not share their feelings. With the usual reluctance of doctors everywhere to take care of their own families, he had arranged with the CMO in Nuku'alofa that I would go there for my confinement. I was to travel down not on the dirty, rolling, old *Hifofua*, but on one of the big copra boats that offered clean, comfortable quarters and a smooth trip. However, just a few months before I was due to go, the rhinoceros beetle was discovered in Vava'u. This almost fist-sized insect with a head that is a replica of the animal for which it is named threatened to destroy the whole way of life of every Vava'u man, woman, and child. In this one-crop country, the coconut provides bread and butter, clothes and shelter, education and amusement. By eating the new growth out of the centre of a tree, the rhinoceros beetle destroys it and with it, its owner's livelihood. Naturally enough, the rest of the kingdom did not want the beetle to spread. Against the pest that infected Vava'u, numerous restrictions arose. Everything that was shipped out had to go into a fumigation shed for twenty-four hours before sailing time. All private shipping between Vava'u and the rest of the kingdom was banned. That meant that not only would the many small boats which used to ply between the groups be forbidden to come to Vava'u, but also that the copra boats, once they had touched here, could visit no other Tongan port. If I wanted to go to Nuku'alofa, I had no choice of transport except the government owned *Hifofua* or the *Aoniu*.

I very much did not want to go to Nuku'alofa. The eighth month of pregnancy is not, under any conditions, the ideal time to travel. The mere thought of the *Hifofua* or the *Aoniu* made me shudder. I suppose, too, I had listened to the village women long enough to absorb their ideas about the convenience of home deliveries. I had, too, been spoiled by having a doctor on the premises. Farquhar, however, insisted that he did not want to go on being my doctor. When I told Anaise, the old woman who did our laundry, that I would probably have to go to Nuku'alofa for the baby's birth, she asked me why. I explained that it was Farquhar's wish.

"Doesn't he know how to do babies?" she asked, and, without waiting for an answer, volunteered, "If he doesn't, I do. I'll do the baby for you!"

Our village cemetery is full of little graves that have been filled by village midwives working with rusty scissors and unclean bandages, so I was not prepared to accept her offer. But, I did want to stay in Vava'u. Poor Farquhar had little peace! I bombarded him with lurid pictures of the dangers of slipping and falling on the *Hifofua's* filthy rolling decks. I pointed to the sunset children and reminded him that they had all been born here in 'Utulei. I talked of Lutui, the capable MO in charge of the Vava'u hospital who could assist him.

In the end, he gave in. One stormy night in September, Lutui and a Tongan nurse came to 'Utulei, but it was Farquhar himself who delivered our daughter and Tu'ifua who looked at once to see that she had the right number of fingers and toes.

We named her Tu'ifua for our friend and Ann for Farquhar's favourite sister and having done so, called her Tami, the third of my important people.

Although I was not aware of it at the time, my fourth important person arrived in 'Utulei just three weeks after Tami did. She was born up the hill and her parents were Soko and Felemi. She was their third child and first daughter. They called her Tupoutu'a which usually gets shortened to Tupou.

At the time Tami was born, I had refused old Anaise's services as a midwife, but she must have been fated to bring us a daughter. One Monday when Tami was two years old—a time at which she had just begun to suspect that for the making of mud pies, sinking fingers caressingly into the depths of old Lassie's fur, collecting all the hibiscus blooms within her reach and similar activities, there might be more understanding companions than any of her three parents (three, for Tu'ifua was her third parent from the very beginning of her life), Anaise came down as usual to do the wash. With her she brought her grandniece, a tiny scrap of Tongan femininity called Tupou. She had bright, shoe-button eyes, straight hair pulled up into a knot and tied by a red ribbon and soft brown baby skin. It did not occur to either Farquhar or me to make any closer observation of her that day. Tami, however, sat opposite her on the wash house floor, eyeing and being eyed for half the morning. Apparently they passed the reciprocal test. Long before lunch time, they were playing happily together and had entered into the most wonderful of all life's experiences, sharing things and ideas.

Without anything being said on either side, Tupou soon became a daily fact of life. Most days she came before breakfast and stayed until dark. As the years went by, all the children in the village found their way into the garden and into the house until there were times when the whole place seemed to be one vast playground, but always, no matter who or how many came, Tupou was the one who stayed when the others had gone home to talk over the day with Tami. Tami knew her for a sister the first day she came. Gradually Farquhar and I came to realise we had two daughters. Anaise had been a good midwife after all. She brought our second daughter.

CHAPTER THREE

DID YOU ADOPT HER LEGALLY?

DID YOU adopt her legally? What about her parents? Surely you can't love her in the same way you do Tami? Such questions my *papalangi* friends asked when they heard that Tupou had become our daughter. Tongans—having an old and happy history of adoption saw no reason to ask. Perhaps by answering them here, I can help explain the Tongan point of view.

We did not adopt Tupou legally. The question never arose because according to Tongan law, a child if he be legitimate, can not be legally adopted while its mother lives and Tupou's pretty mother, Soko, is very much alive. The law is, of course, a European conception grafted onto Tongan life. It becomes important only when there is a question of money or property to be inherited and we are as poor in such things as our Tongan neighbours. The girls share alike in the only inheritance we have been able to give them—a healthy happy childhood, a good education, a love of books and music, a capacity for friendship, and an appreciation of this world and of its Maker. If that is not riches enough, then life is not worth living.

If Tongan law forbids adoption of a child whose mother still lives, Tongan custom recognises no such limitations. Adoption has always been an integral part of the social scheme in Polynesia. If a couple has many children and another couple in their family has none—or not enough—they will give them one. It is as simple as that.

But, my *papalangi* friends cry, you don't belong to Tupou's family. By blood or by law, they are correct, but when I said that the village had accepted us, I meant just that. We have been given not the grudging acceptance Americans manage to give neighbours who differ from them in colour and background, but the complete acceptance that a family gives its members. In this modern world there is a great deal of talk about the brotherhood of man. Tongans prove every day that it is possible.

Soko and Felemi gave us Tupou not because they cared so little for her, but because they cared so much. They knew Tami needed a sister and they felt that with us Tupou would have a far better opportunity to receive a good education than she would with them.

Hard though it is for outsiders to understand, there has been no loss in the whole arrangement. There has been only gain. Tupou gained an extra set of parents. So did Tami; for Soko and Felemi have become her people. They have become our people, too—a couple with whom we feel reciprocal trust and reciprocal love.

That's all very well, the objectors cry, but surely you can't love her in the same way as you do Tami who is your own child. That is true. I do not love Tupou in the same way I love Tami. I cannot love any two people in the same way because no two people are exactly the same. Indeed, it seems to me that the capacity to love at all is the capacity to recognise in each individual his unique qualities.

I have two daughters. I love them both.

CHAPTER FOUR

THE QUEEN COMES TO TEA

History is full of magical names, but most often the magic is in direct proportion to the amount of time that has elapsed since the person concerned lived. Those who, in their own day, become myths, are few. One of them was Tonga's Queen Salote Tupou who ruled this country during the first sixteen years of my stay in it.

Long before she went to Queen Elizabeth's coronation and caught the fancy of the press and the world by refusing to be sheltered from a sudden London downpour, Queen Salote had become, in her own land, a story-book queen. Beauty, power, a regal graciousness, a mystic origin—she had all the components of a mythical queen.

Like all other people in the world, Tongans find no difficulty in holding at one and the same time, conflicting beliefs. Accordingly, although they are all Christians and have been for over a hundred years, they continue to believe that their royal family takes its descent from the old Tongan god, Aho'eitu, who once lost his heart to a beautiful girl of the house of Tupou.

To anyone who ever saw Queen Salote, the belief was understandable. She did seem different from other mortals. It was not so much the fact that—powerfully made and perfectly proportioned she stood over six feet tall, as that she carried herself always with the proud assurance of a born ruler. There was, too, always a touch of loneliness about her. It was due, I think, partly to a widow's natural aloneness and partly to the fact that Tongan custom kept her apart from the small daily intimacies which ordinary people share with family and friends.

I had met her briefly during my first days in Tonga, but it was my second meeting with her that was most memorable. She was due, five months after I arrived here, to pay a visit to Vava'u. Knowing that she was intensely interested in the church schools, I had written when I first heard she was coming to ask if she would have afternoon tea at the college, inspect the girls' work and talk to the tutors. Her secretary had replied that she would come on the first Saturday after she arrived in Vava'u. That would have been enough to make the visit a never to be forgotten one, but Farquhar and I had purely personal interest in her coming which to us was even more exciting than entertaining her at tea.

By then, we had decided to be married and as Tongan ministers were not licensed to marry Europeans, we had planned to have Mr. Pauson who, as Queen's chaplain, would be coming with her, perform the ceremony. A certain amount of correspondence and a visit or two from him, had not increased my liking for him—nor was he the sort of man Farquhar could respect. Consequently, I had not confided to him our plans. I had, perforce, written requesting a blank for a European marriage, but I had given no particulars and he had sent it thinking it was for one of the numerous half-castes who are, legally, Europeans. We decided it would be time enough to tell him that we were the couple concerned when he arrived.

We would both have preferred to be married by Lepa, the Tongan head of the church in Vava'u who, calling himself my Tongan father, had all along taken a kindly interest in us and our affairs, but, in spite of the fact that he was a senior minister and was in addition, an uncle of the queen, he could not perform the service.

Tu'ifua had known our plans almost as soon as we did. Even at that early date, she had become what she has ever since remained—my *"pele"* who, as she explains it, is "the friend who really belongs to you, just like your family". With her rare capacity for sharing other people's joy, she was as happy as we were on that afternoon the Queen was expected. The three of us walked down to the wharf to watch the *Hifofua* come in. Our eagerness had made us early. We stood awhile talking quietly, looking at the bright harbour with its encircling hills, but soon we were caught up in the excitement of the day.

The quiet air began to pulse with a rhythmic beat as the school children came marching barefooted to line the sides of the road from the wharf to Veitatalo, the big old house by the post office where royal visitors always stayed. They made a gay rainbow—our own girls in blue, the Catholics in brown, the Mormons in green and the government schools in red. When they were all in place, the band resplendent in scarlet uniforms, their instruments polished to a dazzle, came down between the children playing a gay march which set our feet and hearts to tapping in time. Soon our governor, the Queen's younger son, Prince Tu'ipelehake, arrived and after him the chiefs of Vava'u and the heads of government departments—tall, fine-looking men all of them, dressed in their best *valas* with finely woven mats, *ta'o valas*, tied neatly about their waists. Behind the officials came a great crowd of people, bright with holiday clothes and holiday spirits.

When the band had played again, we could hear, cutting through the silence that followed its last note, the unmistakable thump, thump, clunk, thump; thump, thump, clunk, thump of the *Hifofua*'s asthmatic old engine. The whole crowd held its breath and turned and stared down the harbour to where the sea curved around the hill of 'Utulei. A minute passed, another still minute and another and then the *Hifofua* chugged into sight. Wildly on the big drum the drummer pounded, everyone shouted " Welcome " and shouted again and again until the whole harbour echoed it—and she was there, the Queen herself, standing up on the bridge waving and smiling.

As the ship docked, the band played and the children sang the songs they had prepared. When they had finished, the Queen and her aide came down the gangway and were met by the official party. They talked together for a few minutes and then the Queen turned and faced the band, standing silent with head slightly bowed as if in prayer. The prayer came—the great swelling notes of the Tongan national anthem which burst from the band and from the throat of every local Tongan, young and old.

    'E 'Otua Mafimafi
    Ko ho mau 'Eiki koe
    Ko koe ko e falala'anga
    Mo e 'ofa ki Tonga
    'Afio hifo 'emau lotu
    'A ia 'oku mau fai ni
    Mo ke tali ho mau loto
    'O malu'i 'a Tupou.

Oh almighty God above,
Thou art our Lord and sure defence;
In our goodness we do trust Thee
And our Tonga Thou dost love;
Hear our prayer for, though unseen,
We know that Thou hast blest our land;
Grant our earnest supplication,
Guard and save Tupou, our Queen.

When it was finished, she moved across to the waiting car, got in and was driven slowly up the wharf road and along to Veitatalo. As she went, the crowd closed behind her and followed along after the car cheering and calling greetings, but Farquhar clasped my hand and whispered, " Now the others will come off," and he and Tu'ifua and I moved closer to the ship.

" The Queen's *matabule*—her talking chief," Tu'ifua whispered as a tall man came down. As the other members of the royal entourage followed, she continued to inform us who they were. " Her nurse, Ofa, her hairdresser, the noble Ve'ehala." One by one she pointed out all the important people. At any other time it would have been fascinating but now Farquhar said impatiently, " Where's Pauson?" And Tu'ifua voicing the obvious replied, " He's not coming yet."

" I suppose he's been sick," Farquhar said with more disgust than sympathy.

At that moment, Tu'ifua grasped my arm, " Look," she said, " That's Uesile Taufa coming down now."

Uninterested I asked, " Who's he?"

" The Queen's Tongan Chaplain."

Her words brought to our minds a fear which soon became a certainty. Tu'ifua had moved across to Uesile as he came on to the wharf, caught hold of his sleeves, and had a whispered conversation. When she returned to me, she said dismally, " Mr. Pauson didn't come."

The Queen's visit was no longer a festive event. Colour and excitement drained out of the day. Slowly, the three of us walked back to my little house on the college grounds.

" What do we do now?" I asked as we sank into chairs in the living room.

Farquhar shrugged his shoulders and said nothing. Tu'ifua offered, " What about Father Gregory?" but she knew even as she made the suggestion that it was useless. We were not Catholics.

We sat and stared at one another disconsolately until Farquhar, trying to raise our spirits, laughed wryly and said, "To think of being in such despair because Pauson didn't come. I suppose the Queen couldn't stand him either!"

Tu'ifua and I laughed perfunctorily. Then, suddenly, she sat upright. "I know," she said, "everything will be all right."

"How can it be?" we wailed in unison.

"You know Johnny Kamea?" she asked.

We knew him very well. He was a carpenter. He had made some shelves for Farquhar's library and was, even then, making some alterations in the house at 'Utulei. We knew, too, that on Sundays he was the Seventh Day Adventist Missionary (and it *is* on Sundays in Tonga. So that we will be in step with our neighbour, New Zealand, the International Date Line juts out of its rightful course to include Tonga. Adventists, not recognising the jutting, contend that Tonga's Sunday is really Saturday and so they observe it as their Sabbath day).

"We know him," we said, "but he's a Tongan. He can't marry us any more than Lepa can."

"Oh, yes, he can," Tu'ifua contradicted gaily. She went on to explain that Johnny had spent some time in Fiji and that while he was there he had been licensed to marry Europeans.

"I'd like that, if he can do it," Farquhar said seriously. "Johnny is a fine man. I'd a lot rather have him marry us than have Pauson."

"So would I," I agreed. The day began to grow festive again. I chortled. "Won't Pauson be pleased to have the headmistress of his college married by an Adventist!" A picture of that sectarian little man with his close pursed lips rose into my mind.

Soon Farquhar went around to see Johnny and discovered that it was as Tu'ifua had said. He could marry us and would be happy to do so. We had a full weekend ahead of us. On Friday afternoon, Farquhar and I would be married. On Saturday, the queen would come to the college for afternoon tea.

Both of us wanted a simple wedding and that is what we had, with Tu'ifua acting as bridesmaid and Lepa, my Tongan father, giving me away and only my college tutors as guests. The ceremony took place in the living-room of my house on the college

C

grounds. When it was over, we all walked around the corner to where John Galloway, Farquhar's landlord and a leading member of Johnny's church, had prepared a feast for us. It was a friendly little gathering with everyone offering us their best wishes while Farquhar and I felt that they had already come true.

When the feast was over, the tutors, led by Tu'ifua, escorted us down to the boat. An evening breeze had sprung up and, as we pushed off from the wharf, I looked up into Tu'ifua's great brown eyes which sparkled a blessing down on us.

" If it hadn't been for Tu'ifua . . ." I said for the first of many times and for the first of many times Farquhar agreed. Then he smiled at me, started the outboard and we sped across the harbour to our home in 'Utulei.

Our wedding night was a proper introduction to the lot of a doctor's wife. We were still sitting on the veranda watching a full moon silver the harbour, listening to the distant muted voices of people passing in boats and the closer sounds of villagers on the beach and savouring our happiness when there was a discreet cough at the far end of the veranda, followed by a very determined knocking.

" Who's there?" Farquhar called out.

" I, Lutui," came the answer as the head MO at the hospital strode into sight.

" Well, hello," Farquhar began, but Lutui interrupted.

" I know, Doctor, I know. I'm sorry to come tonight, but a woman's just been brought in. She's an ectopic, I think, and she's in pretty bad shape. If you could come . . ."

But before he had finished, Farquhar was down the veranda, opening the front door. " Just let me get my stethoscope and some tobacco and I'll be with you," he called over his shoulder.

In a moment, he was back. " How did you come down?" he asked Lutui.

When he said, " With some villagers in a row boat," Farquhar handed him the keys to the engine house and said " We'll take my boat back. If you'll put the engine in, I'll be with you in a minute."

Lutui took the keys and went across the garden to the engine house and Farquhar turned to me. " I'm sorry," he said, " but it can't be helped. Now you know you're a doctor's wife." He leaned down and kissed me and then he followed Lutui down the steps.

A minute later I heard—as I was to do so often in the years to come—the engine spin into action, roar past the house and then grow fainter and fainter until at last there was silence and I knew it had reached the wharf on the other side of the harbour. Laughing at my rueful feelings, I went into the house.

By the next afternoon, the patient was resting easily and Farquhar and I—he in his long white trousers and starched white jacket, I in my best dress, were sitting in the living-room of my house on the college grounds talking to Lepa and his wife, 'Uluakimata, who had come to help us with our tea for the queen.

From outside came the voices of college girls, singing snatches of the song they had prepared for the queen or shouting to one another in the high-pitched excitement that I have come to know is peculiar to Tongans expecting a royal visit. Tu'ifua, in a new dress, wearing the fine linen-like mat which has been handed down in her family for over two centuries, filled the air with a delightful smell of sandalwood as she darted into the living-room to give a finishing touch to a bowl of flowers, or out to the kitchen for a last minute inspection of the cakes and sandwiches—or off to the grounds to see the final rehearsal of the *ma'ulu'ulu*, the famous old Tongan sitting dance which the girls were to do for the queen.

I called Limu and Silia, the two college girls who had been selected to serve, and, with Farquhar playing queen, we went over and over the whole process of afternoon tea. Limu, who thought a betrousered ruddy-faced Scotchman passing as queen a great joke, giggled her way through approaching him, bowing low, and offering an imaginary cup of tea or passing an illusory sandwich; but the practice was a good one, and, when they had run through it a couple of times, I prided myself that they served as skilfully as the Queen's own girls. We were still passing a final empty cup of non-existent tea when Tu'ifua came hurrying inside the room.

"It's two-thirty," she announced. "She'll be here in a minute or two. She's always on time." She cast a critical eye on us and asked, "Are you ready?" We were, but something in Tu'ifua's look sent Farquhar into the bedroom to run a comb through his hair and me following after him to have a final look in the mirror.

When we returned to the living-room, Lepa and 'Uluakimata

who had been sitting with us during the serving lesson had moved from their chairs and were sitting on the floor on either side of the doorway.

I started to ask them why, but Tu'ifua said quickly, " It is our custom," and herself sat on the floor at my side.

At three she stood up and paced across the room and out onto the veranda where she could see up and down the street. " I don't understand it," she said coming in again at the front door. " She's always on time."

Farquhar was helpful. " It's probably just a mistake. Two-thirty is early for afternoon tea. She probably thought you meant three-thirty."

" Perhaps," I said doubtfully, " but she was to inspect the school and see the dances first."

Agreeing with Farquhar, Tu'ifua swept my doubts aside. " You're perfectly right, Toketa. That's it. There's been a mistake about the time."

Fortified by that hope, we set ourselves to wait again, but at four o'clock, Lepa stretched his legs, yawned, and stood up. " Maybe someone came and she was held up," he said. " We'll go home now." And with that, he and 'Uluakimata left.

Tu'ifua watched them until they had disappeared down the garden path. " I think we'd better wait a while longer," she said.

From the kitchen where they were surreptitiously nibbling on cookies, Lima and Silia let forth a cascade of giggles.

I sighed, " What a way to spend the first day of my marriage."

Farquhar laughed at my mournful voice. " Perhaps that will teach you to entertain royalty," he said.

Tu'ifua had been the most patient one of us all, but at five o'clock, she suddenly rose, walked purposefully to the kitchen and burst into a spate of Tongan which sent Limu and Silia running out onto the grounds calling on the girls to weave fresh coconut frond baskets.

" What's going on?" I asked.

" We've waited long enough," she said firmly and went on to explain. " In our custom, if you prepare something for an important person, as we have prepared tea for the Queen today, you wait and when you've waited so long that you know she won't be coming, you send it to her."

It seemed to me a bit like saying, " Here's your old tea . . . and so what?" but as Tu'ifua assured me that it was the polite and accepted thing to do, we bundled sandwiches and cookies, cakes and bottles of lemonade—and even a thermos or two of tea, into baskets. When they were all filled, a group of blue-uniformed girls led by one of the tutors was dispatched to Veitatalo to take the Queen her afternoon tea. Tu'ifua went off to prepare for evening study hall and Farquhar and I returned to 'Utulei. So ended our first attempt to entertain Queen Salote.

Of course, there was an explanation—the simplest—and, from a Tongan point of view, the most natural one in the world. Ve'ehala, the personable young noble who acted as the Queen's social secretary, gave it when he called on us next morning. " You see," he said, " Her Majesty heard about your wedding and she thought you wouldn't be thinking about the tea party. She sends her apologies. She really never thought you'd be there."

" We were there," I said rather huffily. " We agreed to be there and we were," but Farquhar, more agreeably, and in perfect Tongan form said;

" Thank you for coming to tell us."

Ve'ehala smiled. " Her Majesty wanted me to ask if she could come next Saturday instead."

So, when Saturday came round again, my cottage and the college were once more in sparkling order. Once more Farquhar, Tu'ifua and I were dressed in our best clothes, once more Lepa and 'Uluakimata sat on the floor by the door, once more the girls practised serving. As Limu was demonstrating how she would offer the Queen a second cup of tea, the scrawny yellow cat who had adopted me leapt hopefully at the empty tray she held out. " *Pusi kovi* . . . bad cat," shouted Limu as she brought the tray down on the unfortunate animal's head.

" Here, here," I said. " If you do that when the Queen's here, the tea will scald the cat and then you'll have a scene."

Limu tried to look contrite, but laughed in spite of herself. Not a bit amused, Tu'ifua turned to Silia. " Get rid of the cat," she ordered. " Put it somewhere."

At that moment the clock struck the half hour. Two-thirty. We heard a car door close and looked out to see Vilai, the Queen's tall handsome half-brother who served as her aide, going around to hand her out of the car.

Silia and Limu dashed from the room carrying a bewildered

piece of protesting yellow fur between them. Tu'ifua sank to the floor beside Lepa and 'Uluakimata and Farquhar and I went to the veranda to greet our royal guest.

Queen Salote had that greatest of royal social gifts—the ability to make everyone she met feel immediately at ease. She came up the steps that day and onto the veranda and stretching out one hand to Farquhar and one to me, offered us, all in one breath, congratulations on our marriage and apologies for having failed to come the week before.

Her clear, rather deep voice was musical, and musical, too, was her laughter which cascaded through the conversation all that afternoon. But not at all musical was the muffled " Meow, meow, meow," which, as soon as we had stepped into the living-room, came to our ears. I looked around, but I could see no sign of my cat. The Queen had perfect hearing. Fortunately she also had perfect manners. She gave not the slightest sign of having heard anything amiss. Nevertheless, I was relieved when, very shortly, we set out on a tour of the college grounds and left the " Meows " behind.

The three Wesleyan girls' colleges—Queen Salote in Nuku'alofa, Pilolevu in Ha'apai and Siuilikutapu here in Vava'u were especially dear to the Queen's heart. Certainly, she never seemed happier than when she was walking among the girls, seeing examples of their school work and listening to their young voices. She looked that day at countless notebooks, endless embroidered pillowcases and piles of mats and baskets.

Interested as she was in everything belonging to her country's past, she was especially pleased that the traditional crafts of weaving and *tapa* making were being taught in the schools. Now and again, she would reach out with the big fan she always carried, tap a basket and say, " That is beautiful! See the fine even weaving!" or looking at a piece of *tapa*, she would exclaim, " That's a delightful pattern." As she spoke, the face of some one of the blue-uniformed girls standing at attention behind their work, would light up like a tree full of Christmas candles and I would know who had made the item.

When we returned to the house, the girls had put three chairs on the back veranda. There we sat—the Queen and Farquhar and I—she in the middle in a big *tapa*-draped armchair and Farquhar and I on either side of her with Tu'ifua, Lepa and 'Uluakimata on the floor at our feet. When we were settled, Tu'ifua leaned toward the Queen and told her the college had prepared some songs and dances for her. She nodded her head, smiled and said, "Let them begin."

A sitting dance may sound like a contradiction in terms, but everyone who has seen the *ma'ulu'ulu* knows that it is not. There was something delightfully incongruous about the double line of thirty girls who, dressed in the college blue jumper and white blouse, had tied brightly-coloured grass skirts about their waists, dyed their cheeks with red hibiscus and hung frangipani *leis* (garlands) about their necks. They came up before us, stopped, bowed low to the Queen and, sitting down, spread out their gay grass skirts and listened attentively for the first beat of the drum behind them. When it came, every arm was outstretched as with shoulders, arms, hands and heads, the girls began to dance. The lower part of their bodies remained still except for a tell-tale bare toe or two beating time to the music.

"That's a very old dance," the Queen said to me, "so old that no-one now knows what the words mean."

I nodded and she continued, "There are many such. Some of them must go back to the distant time when all the Polynesians were one people in some Asiatic homeland."

On a long-drawn-out plaintive note, the *ma'ulu'ulu* finished. The girls stood up, bowed again, and marched away. Although Siuilikutapu was a girls' college, we had one class of boys who lived on some church property just out of town and came into classes every day. Not at all chagrined at belonging to a girls' school and not to be outdone by the girls, either, they had demanded permission to do a dance. Now they came in, tripping over the anklets that they all wore which were made of the big flat seeds called *pa'anga* which clacked as they walked. They had skirts of leaves and were bare from the waist up except for leaf collars. Each boy carried a long spear. They may have come bumbling in in the clumsy way typical of adolescent boys everywhere, but once they started to dance, they moved in a rhythm as perfect as the girls' had been, but what a different rhythm it was! The spear dance goes back to the old days when war parties danced themselves into a frenzy to give themselves courage for battle. It is a favourite with young boys, for as they dance and thrust their spears with a violence that makes one fear for their lives, but with such perfect control that they never actually touch one another, they give forth fearful blood-curdling yells.

"There's no question about their being healthy young specimens if they can stand up to that," Farquhar said.

The Queen held her fan to her ears and laughed. "How noisy they are, but how they love it!"

And noisy they were, but not noisy enough to drown out a "Me—o—w" that seemed drawn out of pure fury.

"In the old days," said the Queen quickly, "the spears were beautifully carved and inlaid with shell."

"Me—o—w, meow, meow."

"I know," I replied. "I saw some fine ones in the museum in Auckland."

When the last of the dances was finished, the Queen stood and for a few minutes spoke to the students who filled the square in front of us. She introduced Farquhar formally and spoke of her joy at our marriage. She thanked the dancers and expressed her interest in the college work she had seen. She spoke of the future and of the young people there that day who would help to create it and asked God's blessing on them all. Then, with Tu'ifua holding the door, she went through to the living-room. Farquhar followed her, but I lagged behind to whisper to Tu'ifua, "Where's that cat?" for the Queen's speech had been heavily punctuated with feline remarks.

"I don't know," she said hopelessly and then, as I showed signs of lingering to find out, she gave me a push and whispered, "Go on. You can't stay out here."

So in I went and when we were all seated, I gave the nod that had been agreed on as a signal for Limu and Silia to start serving tea. Out of the corner of my eye, I saw them leave the kitchen and cross the dining-room carrying, each one, her tray at just the proper angle. I had not finished congratulating myself on having such well-trained girls when they stepped into the room, took one terrified look at the Queen and fled—to the inevitable "meow". The Queen fanned herself busily. Tu'ifua rose and went into the kitchen. When she came back into the room, she was carrying a tray. "Come and help," she said to me. "Those wretched girls were frightened. They've run away."

So much for our practices! Tu'ifua and I managed very well. She, Lepa and 'Uluakimata, in accordance with Tongan custom, would not eat in the presence of the Queen so there were only three of us to be served. And soon we were all provided with sandwiches, cakes and tea. The Queen had just asked Farquhar something about the Medical Department when, as if it rose from under our very feet, came another anguished " meow ".

The Scotch are noted for facing issues squarely and for saying what must be said. Brushing aside the Queen's polite unconcern and my studied indifference, Farquhar lived up to his national characteristics. " Where," he demanded in a loud voice, " is that cat and what is wrong with it?"

My thoughts were scarcely those of a loving bride. I felt my cheeks flush scarlet as I replied miserably, " I don't know. I think the girls put it somewhere so it wouldn't be in the way."

From behind the Queen's fan came a delighted titter. " Maybe they'd better let it out," she suggested; so Farquhar and I finished serving tea while Tu'ifua went off to find Limu and Silia and discover where they had put the cat.

When the tea was finished, I asked the Queen if I might present my tutors to her. She said at once that she'd like that. In my mind, I had made a picture of that part of the afternoon. It was, I suppose, based on American faculty meetings called to hear some famous visiting educator in which, following introductions, the visitor spoke and the faculty asked questions. It was not to be. I had made my mental picture without taking Tongan custom into consideration.

Tu'ifua came back about that time and the Queen looked up at her and said, " Well, where was the cat?"

" In the woodbox."

" Poor thing! " the Queen said and then, to Tu'ifua, " Come and sit beside me." I watched as she sank to the floor beside the royal feet.

The next tutor was an island girl who had never been so close to the Queen before. As I called her name, she came to the doorway of the room, sank to the floor, crawled on hands and knees across the mat, seized one of the Queen's bare feet in her hands, fondled it for a minute and then bent and laid her cheek against it.

When I saw that, I forgot all about American faculty meetings. We were in fact, witnessing the ancient ceremony of *moemoe'i* accorded in times past only to the Tu'itonga, the spiritual ruler of

Tonga. As Queen Salote was a descendant of the last Tu'itonga she was, in Tongan eyes, entitled to such signs of respect.

As one after another of the tutors repeated the same performance, all my American ideas of equality rose into my mind—and yet, there was something perfectly natural about the whole thing as if, in that moment of contact with their ruler each of those young tutors was joining herself with the whole stream of her country's history and ideals. It was a shared moment—as moving, I think, to the Queen as to the tutors.

When the last of them had been presented, they sat in a circle on the floor about the Queen while she thanked them for their work in the college. She spoke, as she was to do so often again in the future of the difficult time of transition that lay ahead as Tonga moved from being a small isolated agricultural country to take its place in the great family of nations. She stressed the role education had to play in the coming changes and implored the tutors, as she was later to implore all Tongans to " Keep the best of your own old Tongan ways and adopt the best of the new European ways."

She came to an end, looked up, pointed across the room with her fan. " There's the culprit."

I followed her gaze to where my scraggy yellow cat sat in the doorway exercising the old feline prerogative of looking at a queen.

" *Si'i pusi* . . . poor kitty," she said as, still laughing, she rose and said it was long past time for her to be going.

Farquhar, Tu'ifua and I, followed by the cat, saw her to the car. We were not alone. Crowding behind us were the tutors and the college boys and girls. They were completely silent until Queen Salote lowered the window at her side, leaned out and called, " Thank you again—all of you." Then they set up a great cheer which must have echoed in her ears all the way back to Veitatalo.

CHAPTER FIVE

AS THE TWIG IS BENT...

That of all my tutors, Tu'ifua was the one that Queen Salote knew was no mere coincidence. Her family has long been distinguished for its loyalty to the house of Tupou and for its devotion to all things Tongan, and her father, Fevale'aki, was an outstanding worker in the church that meant so much to the Queen.

Fevale'aki was unlike any other Tongan I ever knew. A tall man, thin by local standards, he wore his close-cropped white hair limed in the old-fashioned manner so that it stood upright, adding to his height and to the dignity that was an integral part of him. His habitual expression was solemn, but he had a deep appreciation of life which often made him smile in delight and a ready wit which could crinkle his face into laughter. When I first knew him, he was already an old man whose days of working in the bush were almost over. He did not, however, spend his time in the endless rounds of kava-drinking so dear to most aged Tongan men, but in a completely a-typical fashion stayed at home and read and wrote. I used to wonder when I saw him filling page after page with his neat copperplate writing what sort of childhood he and his gentle wife, Kau'ata, had provided for Tu'ifua and her brothers and sisters.

One day Tu'ifua and I were walking down the beach here at 'Utulei when we came across a group of village children—the oldest scarcely more than a baby, splashing in and out of the water.

"What are their parents thinking of?" Tu'ifua asked sternly. "They should send someone with these children to watch them."

I laughed at her pompous manner. "I suppose when you were that age you were doing the same thing."

Her brown eyes flashed. "I certainly was not—not with my father," and then she told me of her childhood.

As a young man, Fevale'aki had been a school inspector. By the time his own children came along, he had very definite ideas about raising the young—ideas which, I think, would have delighted Maria Montessori.

Around his large garden, he planted a hedge. Inside the garden, he planted all the trees and shrubs and small plants for which Tongans have found a use. There were fruit trees such as mangoes, bananas, custard apples, oranges, lemons and sour sops as well as all the island vegetables—*talo* and yam, breadfruit and *kape*. Trees whose bark was used for medicine, he planted and all the sweet smelling things from which Tongans make oil to rub on their skin or whose blooms they pick to string into *leis*.

That garden was the kindergarten and first school of Tu'ifua, her brothers, sisters, and cousins. There they learned of all the riches with which their land has been blessed. They learned, too, of the Christian way of life. A deeply religious man, Fevale'aki gathered the children about him every morning. He read to them from the Scriptures and they sang a hymn together. Then they went into the garden where they spent the long sunny days of childhood. Sometimes he took them out into the bush lands and taught them the names of the forest trees and told them what they were used for. Sometimes they went to the beach where they learned about the creatures of the sea.

"But we never went alone like those children we saw down on the beach," Tu'ifua said. "Fevale'aki believed that children should be watched and taught and studied all the time."

If Tu'ifua's father's programme for children was rigorous, it was tempered by Kau'ata, her mother, whose unfailing patience and kindness seem all directed toward making children happy.

"Kau'ata made us horns and whistles from coconut fronds," Tu'ifua said, "and she taught us how to string shells and flowers to make *leis*. When we were tired of playing, she and Fevale'aki told us the old stories of the Tongan people and they taught us about our family so we would know our own people."

At the end of those long days of childhood, the father once more gathered the children about him. He invited them to consider each one, his own behaviour during that day. Had he been honest? Had he been kind? Had he acted like a worthy Tongan?

Sometimes he spoke of the lifelong duty that they had to help people less fortunate than themselves and to lead the community into better ways of living. Always the day ended as it had begun with a Bible reading and a hymn.

Fevale'aki is dead now and the children he guided so carefully are all grown up—some of them with children and grandchildren of their own. I have come to know them all—a governor, a judge, doctors, church and civic leaders—one and all they have proved to be the very sort of people Fevale'aki hoped to raise when he planted his garden long ago.

CHAPTER SIX

AT HOME IN 'UTULEI

SEEN FROM the deck of the monthly steamer, our house looks much the same as it did on that morning when I first sailed into Vava'u harbour, but it has grown and changed with the passing years just as we have done. The first change took place shortly after we were married. Farquhar was renting the house then from John Galloway. John's mother had been an 'Utulei woman, but he got his Scotch name and Scotch blood from his father, a ship's carpenter who long ago jumped ship here and, cutting off all his old home bonds, made for himself a new life in Vava'u. The point on which the house stands is named for him, although I think that few of the people who read the chart realise when they see Point Kalue that " Ka—lu—e " is merely the Tongan spelling for the good Scotch Galloway.

When, in the early days of our marriage, we sat on the veranda looking down the harbour and considered the beauty of the world about us and the contentment we felt within ourselves, we felt we wanted this place to be ours forever. Renting seemed a precarious, unsatisfactory arrangement. We wanted the security of ownership. Fortunately for us, as John's wife much preferred living in Neiafu, he agreed to sell and soon we could call the house, with all the pride of new possession, our home.

That first and most important change was the only one that took place during our first year. Because I was still at the college and had to continue to live there and Farquhar was called to Nuku'alofa for some months to take the place of the CMO who had gone on leave, the house was, for months, only a weekend cottage to which I went, sometimes alone, sometimes with Tu'ifua. Not until December when my year at the college was completed and Farquhar had returned to Vava'u, did we really begin to live in 'Utulei.

It was larger than the other village houses, but it followed the same general pattern of all Tongan built timber dwellings—a central box with surrounding verandas. The library, living-room, front bedroom and *loki veve* formed the central box. The bathroom, kitchen, dining alcove and back bedroom had simply been built into the back and side veranda.

The house stands on piles and in those early days, you climbed a rickety flight of stairs to reach the veranda. It was—and is, the glory of the place. Running clear across the front and down one side of the house, it follows the curve of the sea around the point so that wherever you are on it, you have a view of the harbour. On the side veranda which is only about fifteen feet from the water, you can hear, at high tide, the lap of the waves against the shore and, on still nights, the sudden splash of fish jumping.

It was only when we opened the door and went into the living-room that we began to realise what a strange old shell of a place we had bought. The basic framework was made of good sound *kauri* from New Zealand, but the rest of it John had built from scraps. Many of the rooms were still unlined. No two windows matched and no doors or walls anywhere in the whole place were on the square. This meant that when we turned ourselves into carpenters—which we did very soon, Farquhar and I were constantly trying, not as ordinary workers do, to true up our boards, but to set them at the correct angle to correspond to the existing deviations.

If John had been something less than a builder, Farquhar was something less than a decorator. In the year that he had lived alone in the house, the problem of furniture had scarcely concerned him. There was none at all in the living room which served mainly as a passage-way to other rooms and as a convenient place to leave things you didn't happen to want at the minute. In the dining alcove, there was a table and some chairs and in the kitchen, a stove and a kerosene refrigerator. There was a bed in the bedroom and across one corner hung a piece of island print cloth to make a clothes closet.

The room next to the front bedroom was one which John had reserved when he rented the house to Farquhar. In it, he kept broken lamps, old bottles, bits of chipped window glass, old letters and papers and similar debris. We began at once to call it *loki veve*, the rubbish room. As soon as we had bought the house, I began a long campaign to get John to move his things away. When he finally did, we used the room to store things that " might be useful someday ". Before long, it contained again broken lamps, old bottles, bits of chipped window glass, old letters and papers and similar debris. To add to its hectic condition, Farquhar soon acquired a set of carpenter's tools and set up a workshop in one corner. The first thing we taught the girls who came to work for us, was to keep the door of *loki veve* shut at all times—particularly when company was coming, but there was always a tell-tale trickle of sawdust leaking out from under it.

In all the house, it was only the library that was completely furnished. There, in his bachelor days, Farquhar had spent most of his time at home. Johnny Kamea and some of the village men had lined the room with shelves and given it a coat of fresh white paint. There was a couch whose green and white cover matched the curtains, a comfortable wicker chair, and the big old armchair which Farquhar's New Zealand patients had given him when he set out for the islands. Beside the armchair stood a chest to hold the radio and on the other side of the room was a desk. The most important library furniture—the books, Farquhar had been collecting all his life. There was the set of Lamb and the Goldsmith which he had won as class prizes at Hutcheson's Grammar School in his native Glasgow and the Hippocrates that marked his medical school days at the University of Glasgow. His prized Pepys books filled one section and an assortment of military volumes and a wonderful selection of English literature covered the back wall. It was not long before my own books arrived from California and made it necessary to build more shelves. That has been a recurring activity because—happily, the library never stops growing.

Privacy is no part of Tongan life and the village people saw no reason why it should be of ours, either. Nor did they see any reason why, since Farquhar had come to live in 'Utulei, they should go across the harbour to the hospital when they were sick. They regarded him as the resident physician of the village and long before I came to 'Utulei, had turned the front veranda into a waiting room. In the mornings before I had opened my eyes, I used to hear the village sick climbing the stairs, walking back and

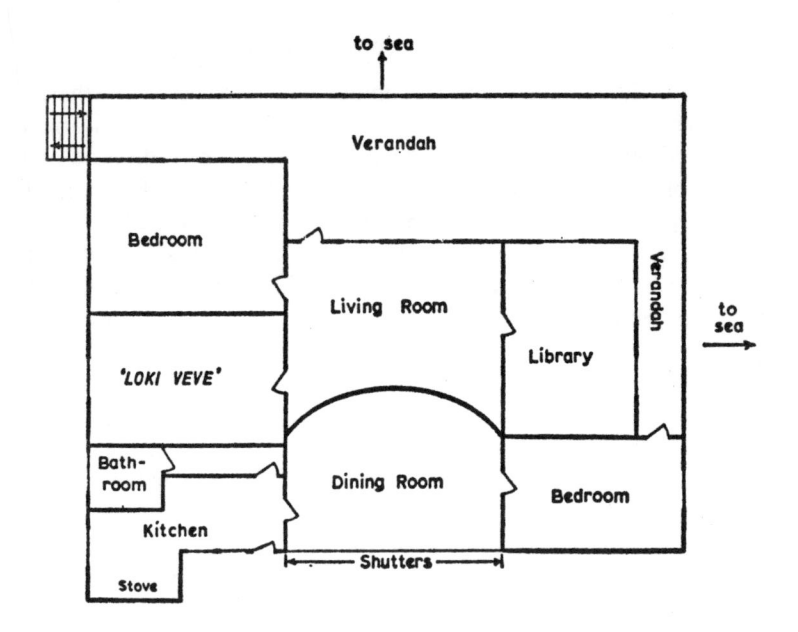

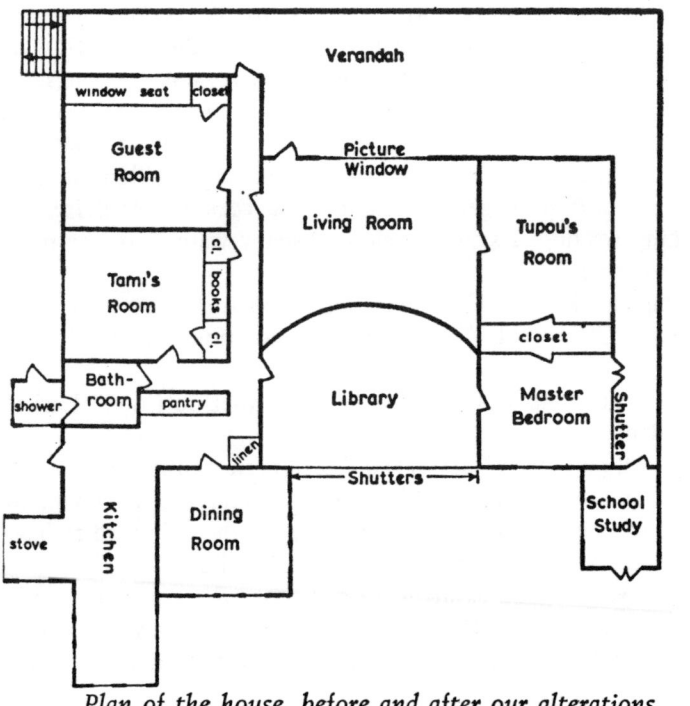

Plan of the house, before and after our alterations

forth on the veranda and coughing. The coughs were sharp, persistent, and invariably preceded by a lengthy and noisy clearing of the throat. Lest anyone conclude that respiratory diseases are more common in Tonga that elsewhere in the world, I hasten to say they are not. It is only that there are no doorbells in this country and a persistent cough is the accepted substitute. If Farquhar had not got up and gone to see them before their throats were dry from coughing, they would simply walk back to our bedroom window stick their heads in and call, " Toketa, Toketa, are you there, Toketa?" He had grown used to them, but suspecting that I would never do so, I moved our bedroom to the back. Later still, we put a lattice screen with a door that locked on the end of the veranda and the waiting room was forced to move to the wash house we had built beyond the kitchen.

The biggest structural change we made in the house was a present from my brother-in-law, Willie Matheson, who over the years has been our most frequent visitor. Having lived as a young man in Samoa for some years, Willie understood the domestic problems peculiar to the islands. " Everything in the tropics ", he used to say, " is worn out, broken or rusted ". Often enough I have recognised the truth of his words. Another irritation of tropical living that was hard to get used to was the bugs. In California, it is only dirty people who are overrun by cockroaches. Here they are everywhere. One day Willie came into the kitchen where the house girl and I were busy scrubbing the floor as hard as we could. " We'll get rid of those old cockroaches if it's the last thing we do," I said as I sloshed soapy water into the most remote corners.

Willie chuckled. " They love nothing better than nice clean damp wood," he said, " and scorpions and stink bugs revel in it, too."

I could not match his merriment. " So what do I do?" I asked despondently.

" I'll tell you what," he replied. " I've been wanting to give you people something that would be really useful and now I know what it will be—a cement kitchen. They are the only kind to have in the tropics. I'll give you the money to build one."

Willie was as good as his word and soon we were immersed in kitchen plans. We decided to keep the old kitchen and turn it into a much-needed cupboard room and so it has remained. While acting as passageway from the new kitchen to the rest of the house, it now contains the linen cupboard, the pantry, a storage for flower containers and chinaware and a laundry drop.

I forget who recommended Taniela to us as an expert cement worker. Under the circumstances, it is just as well I do. To be sure, he had learned to put a cement wall together, although anyone who looks at the kitchen can see that the wall wavers uncertainly in places. He had learned, too, the desirability of steady wages and having got the job with us was determined to make it last as long as possible. The obvious way to do that was to stretch the work out by fair means or foul.

In the mornings before Farquhar left for the hospital, he was a model of industry, bustling about shouting orders to the two boys who had been hired to help him and even, when he thought someone was watching, picking up a trowel and spreading a bit of mortar himself. But as soon as Farquhar had gone, Taniela had gone, too. He was not so indiscreet as to leave the premises. He merely left off work. At first, so that when I suddenly rounded a corner, he could start puttering with something and pretend to be working, he stayed close to where the two boys were laying bricks. Later he took to going into the workshop, a building we had put up in the back yard to house Farquhar's growing collection of tools and the other contents of *loki veve*. With the shutters down, in pleasant darkness, after a smoke or two, he could drift off to sleep until noon when Farquhar was due back from the hospital. Not surprisingly, the work proceeded very slowly, although every Saturday afternoon, Taniela, wide awake, was waiting with outstretched hand for the week's pay. Beginning to fear that the money would run out long before the building was finished, I burst into the workhouse one morning. There was Taniela lying on the floor snoring in gentle oblivion. I shook him violently and when he woke, stormed, " What do you think you're doing?"

He blinked up at me. " I have a terrible headache," he said and gave me a faint, mocking smile.

" Maybe a little work would help it," I suggested. " Get up and try it."

He groaned. " I couldn't possibly get up." His tone was pitiful, but it did not move me. I slammed the door and went out.

When Farquhar came home from the hospital, I met him on the beach and asked him to go to see Taniela at once.

"Well, has he got a headache?" I demanded when Farquhar came into the house.

"I'm sure I don't know."

"You ought to know. After all, you're a doctor."

Farquhar explained then that although a doctor could very well tell whether a person who claimed to have a backache or an ear ache—or any one of a hundred other kinds of aches—really had it, he could only take his word for a headache. "I can't look inside his head," he said, " or feel inside it. If he says it aches, I must believe him."

"You can believe him if you like," I retorted. "I don't."

Farquhar put his arm around me. "Don't get so upset. Things always take longer than you expect them to," he said.

When, however, day after day passed and the building scarcely rose a course, when Taniela was smitten by his mysterious headache again and again as soon as Farquhar had left in the mornings, I tackled my husband again and finally convinced him that whether the headaches were fact or fiction, it was not economically sound for us to subsidise them any longer. We let Taniela go home to enjoy his ailments in comfort and found a healthier and more honest fellow to finish the job.

The new kitchen jutted out at a right angle to the old one and long before it was finished, I found myself thinking how easy it would be to fit an extra room into that angle. The old dining alcove opened onto the living-room which in turn opened onto the front veranda. Consequently, at every meal time, we were exposed to the coughs of Farquhar's village patients. The idea of having a real dining-room where we could eat in privacy was appealing to both of us. It was accomplished easily by fitting a room into the space between the old kitchen and the new one. By the time that was done, we had spent the money allotted for workers, so Farquhar, Tu'ifua and I put in the floor and the two knotty pine walls and painted the ceiling and the plaster walls a soft yellow. The carpenters' union would undoubtedly have looked askance at the three of us, but we made an efficient, if unorthodox, team. Farquhar did most of the sawing and all of the nailing while Tu'ifua and I performed the necessary function of holding boards in place. When it came to the floor, that meant sitting on them as hard as possible while he nailed.

When both kitchen and dining-room were finished, Willie, who by then was back in Scotland, put the crowning touch on his present by sending us an English slow combustion stove.

A Tongan friend who was staying with us at the time regarded a new kitchen and a new stove as events that could only properly be celebrated with food, so when the stove was in place and the chimney had been set up, she shooed us out of the kitchen and got to work.

As she has the reputation of being one of the best cooks in the kingdom, it was with a definite sense of anticipation that we gathered on the veranda for afternoon tea.

"Oh, look!" shouted Tami and Tupou as the door opened and the biggest, roundest, highest chocolate cake any of us had ever seen was borne in by my beaming friend.

"That stove must have a very good oven," Farquhar remarked with satisfaction as the cake was set triumphantly down on the table.

Tami got her order in at once. "I want an end piece with lots of frosting," and "Me, too," echoed Tupou, but the first piece came to me "because," said my friend, "chocolate is your favourite."

It felt so light and looked so delicious that I had a hard time to keep from sampling it until the others had been served, but I managed to wait and we all bit at once . . . and then,

"It's awful!" I choked.

"Water—quick," shouted the girls and "What did you do to it?" they demanded.

My poor friend, her triumphant smile gone, looked as if she might burst into tears. Instead, she laughed with the rest of us when Farquhar, polite as always, said soberly, "I think a mistake has been made."

It had, indeed. The soda which had made the cake rise to such unbelievable heights was taken from the new package Farquhar had brought home that day. Unfortunately it was not baking soda. It was washing soda!

For a number of changes we made in the house, Tami and Tupou were responsible. During her first five months, Tami slept in our room in a bassinet which Farquhar built from some oak he got from a copra ship. She was a robust little creature and before long her bedtime gymnastics threatened to send the whole structure—bassinet, mosquito net and baby hurtling to the floor. We thought we had defeated her when we wedged the bassinet securely into a corner, but she was the victor. She promptly outgrew it. Up in the village, families sleep together in one room, curling companionably around one another like a litter of puppies. Consequently, when it became known that Tami was to move into a crib and that the crib would be in a separate room, the village for a time, regarded us as unfeeling and unnatural parents. Later they came to accept the idea of separate rooms for children as just one more evidence of *papalangi* foolishness. The room into which she moved was the old *loki veve*. To make that possible, we had thrown away boxes and boxes of rubbish and moved Farquhar's tools and everything else we wanted to keep into the work house in the back yard. When the room was empty, we gave it a coat of paint, hung some bright-coloured linen nursery rhymes on the wall and moved in the crib.

We got her into a room of her own just in time. Before she was a year old, she was running about the house and garden busying herself with collecting wilted flowers, unripe tomatoes, sea shells complete with animals and similar finds which for several trying years were her greatest treasures. We were thankful when, eventually, her attention turned to less odoriferous collections such as dolls, paints and books. Long before she learned to read, we had to build a set of bookshelves into her room. With grandparents in America, aunts and uncles in Scotland, and friends everywhere, she began very soon to acquire an interesting cosmopolitan library. Farquhar and I early developed the habit of reading all her books as well as our own. It was a pleasant way to bring back memories of our own young reading days. We found, too, that the "bigger than life" heroes of children's books and their serious involvement in all the adventures of life were a welcome antidote to the anti-heroes of modern novels whose only reaction to the universe or to themselves is apathy.

When Tupou first became part of our family, she moved into Tami's room with her. They were seven years old then and the joy of being sisters was so great that they felt compelled to room together. A few years later, when each one became more conscious of her own individuality, and, like true sisters, developed differently, they gave me no peace until each had a room of her own . . . nor did they see anything illogical in the fact that, once they had separate quarters, they spent all their time together "visiting" in one room or another.

The girls were responsible, too, for a little building at the foot of the garden right out on the point which came to be known as 'Utulei Beach School. We found early in our school days that school held in a bedroom or in the library or out on the veranda is just not the same as school held in a proper school room. To both teacher and students, there is a certain psychological push about actually going to school. The building was useful, too, in establishing the proper attitude in the villagers. So long as we were in the house or on the veranda, no one in the village saw any good reason why we couldn't be disturbed whenever anyone wanted to borrow the saw, get a recipe, or merely review the local gossip. When we built the school house in the garden, I called a meeting of the village women and explained that school was a very important business and it would be quite impossible for the girls or me to talk about anything while it was going on. Considering that the village school at that time was a casual sort of club which teacher, students and villagers wandered in and out of at will, it is perhaps not surprising that they thought I was making much ado about nothing. However, they nodded solemnly and said, " Io, fine'eiki—yes, mistress ".

" Io fine'eiki " meant, as I was to discover on that and numerous subsequent occasions not " Yes, we agree," but merely " Yes, we hear you."

The first week we held school in the new building, quite as if I'd never said a word about the matter, a few people came down every morning and stood outside the door, coughing and coughing again to let me know they were there. I never discovered what it was they wanted. They might have been thin air for all the attention we paid them. In spite of some suppressed giggles from the girls, we went on with school, talking fast and furiously until the coughs stopped and their owners went away. From then on, our school was undisturbed.

On hot sunny days, the classroom was a delight, cooled by a breeze that swept always around the point, but in bad weather it was dismal. Then the wind howled so that we could scarcely hear ourselves speak and what was worse, it drove the rain in under the shutters. Rivulets ran down the walls and filled the floor with puddles. In such a damp atmosphere teacher and students developed sniffles and books and papers broke out in a bad case of mildew. For some years we endured it, but when the girls were in the eighth grade and needed many more reference books than they had had before, we made the school into a store room and built, at the end of the side veranda, a light, airy room protected from the wind. In it we were able to have a big blackboard on one wall and a solid wall of good, dry bookshelves on another. There, very comfortably, we held all the rest of our classes for as long as 'Utulei Beach School lasted.

Where Farquhar spent his summers of boyhood in the little Highland village of Dornie on the Kyle of Lochalsh, the loch waters were so chilly that swimming was a harrowing ordeal. He never later—not even after he came to 'Utulei and had the best of all swimming pools at the foot of his own garden—developed much interest in the sport. It was very different with the girls and me. In California where I grew up, swimming was definitely considered one of the primary joys of life. Tami and Tupou, like all the other 'Utulei people, were early amphibious. Farquhar's happiness in the sea came from looking at it, or in skimming over its surface in the boat, but Tami and Tupou and I thought no day complete unless we had been into it. In their baby years, before our lives were regulated by school, we were in and out of the sea all day long. Coming up from the beach there were always three trails of wet sand trickling up the steps, along the veranda, through the living-room and down the hall into the bathroom. In order to keep the living-room reasonably dry and also to give it a bit more privacy, I cut a slice off both Tami's room and the front bedroom, which had become the guest room, and made a hall. It was a very useful thing to have, but I soon began to dislike the trail of wet sand in it, too. Then I solved the problem once and for all by having built onto the bathroom a shower with an outside door and a drain big enough to carry away all the sand we could track up.

When we got the new dining-room, the old dining alcove no longer served any useful purpose. It was merely a big empty space at the end of the living-room. Indeed, it was big enough to be the ideal place to move the library which by then had grown so much that books were stacked on every chair and on piles on the floor. The timing was right. It was just then that Tupou and Tami were clamouring for separate bedrooms and the old library would make an ideal room for Tupou. Tu'ifua and I talked about how the alcove could be converted and we drew and redrew plans until we found one that pleased us.

"What do you think of this?" I asked, putting our final plan down in front of Farquhar.

He shook his head helplessly. "You know I can't answer hypothetical questions," he said.

"But this isn't a question and you don't answer it. It's a plan and all you do is say whether you like it or not."

"It's just the same as a hypothetical question," he insisted. "I can't tell until it's finished if I like it or not."

"Try to think about it," I urged, but all he would say was, "If you think that's what you want, we'll build it."

So Tu'ifua and I as executive carpenters with Farquhar and Tupou's father, Felemi, as working ones, transformed the old dining alcove into the new library. Instead of making a solid wall to shut the room off from the living room, we built a high double bookcase with half the books facing out toward the living-room and half in toward the library. This gave us a wall that was truly worth looking at and, in addition, allowed for the free passage of air and light in the spaces above the books. In the library proper, we built a short double shelf and brought in the glassed-in double case that Farquhar had made to house my poetry books. Under the windows parallel to the long double shelf, we made a wide window seat and against the far wall built a spacious desk. When Farquhar's old green armchair and a chair for the desk had been moved in, the room was furnished. We all liked it very much and Farquhar, who had been incapable of visualising it before it was built, adopted it at once as his own special province.

I well realise that most people who live in what we here call "Away", when their family or their fortunes increase, move to a bigger house in a better neighbourhood. We like to feel that a home is for always and that it can grow and change with the people who live in it. Added to that is the conviction we have that, though we were to move a thousand times, we could never anywhere in the world find better neighbours than the 'Utulei villagers. It is true that they cough at our doors, stare at our company, lose our tools and most often think we are mad, but it is equally true that all through the years they have been ready to help us in whatever we have tried to do. They have danced and sung with us in our times of rejoicing and we have wept together in times of sorrow. Can more be asked of neighbours?

Farquhar found carpentry a challenge and a satisfaction. I hoped he would feel the same way about gardening. He did not. He could bend over a board that needed planing for as long as it took to make it true and smooth, but bending over to pull up a weed did, he said, make him ill. In the theoretical side of gardening, he was mildly interested. In what combinations of fertilisers were suitable for which plants and which trace elements had to be added for maximum bloom, he could concern himself but spreading fertiliser was not one of his activities. He indulged willingly enough with me in a brief excursion into hydroponics and when I wanted to try to induce mutations in hibiscus by subjecting the seeds to X-ray, he co-operated by taking them to the hospital laboratory. When the garden was freshly weeded and looking its best, he would conduct guests about it with an air of great satisfaction, but work in it, he would not. The garden was mine and Tu'ifua's.

We had, literally, a clear field to work in. John Galloway had obviously been Farquhar's sort of gardener. When we came to 'Utulei, there was nothing at all growing here except two breadfruit trees, an avocado that John's sister had planted and a scraggy strand tree that had grown by itself.

For a year or two I passed through what can only be called a period of nostalgic gardening during which I tried to make grow here all the vegetables and flowers which flourish around my native San Francisco. For my troubles, I reaped a unique assortment of failures—beautiful long grey-green artichoke foliage, but no artichokes; potatoes that went into the ground and liked it so well that they never came back up; fuchsias whose spindly branches collapsed beneath the weight of their pale leaves and poppies that rotted before they bloomed. Over the years, I have learned that there are a great many things which grow equally well in both California and Vava'u, but in the first years I seemed to try all the impossibles.

Botanists tell us that Tonga, like the other Pacific islands, had originally a very limited flora, but the first Polynesians brought plants from Asia and the early European explorers made contributions from Europe and the Americas. Many of these plants such as papayas, limes and avocados settled in so well that it is hard nowadays to believe they are not native. Everything that will grow in the tropics of either the eastern or the western hemisphere will grow here and a high percentage of sub-tropicals will flourish, too.

As the early comers were practical people who were interested in feeding themselves, most of the plants they brought were food plants. Ornamentals came much later—and are still coming. When I returned from my first trip back to America, I brought from Hawaii pink torch ginger and the flowering banana. Tu'ifua and I have since seen our original plants multiply until they are spread all over the Kingdom. There is a thrill to introducing new plants to a country that is like introducing new ideas to people.

I got my start on tropical plants, as I did on so many other local things, from Tu'ifua. While we were still at the college, she began to tell me the names of the things that grew in the grounds. There I planted a seed of the 'ohai tree—the flamboyant. When I came to live in 'Utulei, I carried the seedling across the harbour in a tin. Now it shades half the lower garden and has branches along which Polito, the yardboy, walks as easily as if he were strolling up a path. At Christmas times its blooms decorate the garden with gold and scarlet. The rest of the year its fern-like foliage shelters the bird's nest ferns and the orchids which Polito has planted high in the forks of its branches.

Tu'ifua contributed not only knowledge about plants, but plants themselves. Fridays when Farquhar came home from the hospital, he always brought her with him for the weekend. When I went down to the beach to meet them, the boat usually looked like a travelling forest. Tree-sized frangipani cuttings, baskets of hibiscus, little plants with their roots carefully tied up in folded breadfruit leaves—Tu'ifua had gathered them all from her own big garden and from the gardens of all her aunts and cousins. It wasn't long before Farquhar was protesting. " Please, please. I don't want to live in a jungle." Had everything we planted grown, he would have been in danger of doing so, but here, as elsewhere, gardening is full of casualties. Even so, his fears were not entirely unjustified. The ground is so fertile and growth during the hot humid rainy season so fast that soon after the garden was established our main job was not putting in, but thinning out, cutting out, pulling up, and so it has been ever since.

With our yardboy pressed into service, Tu'ifua and I made many trips in the boat to nearby reefs where we collected coral with which to line the garden paths and from which to construct raised beds. As soon as the girls were old enough, they came along, too, and splashed merrily in and out of the sea helping us to fill the boat with all the different sorts of coral they could find. The round, hassock-like coral which Tongans call *ponga* makes ideal containers, for African violets, ferns and other plants that like cool moisture. Its hundreds of minute holes are a built-in root cooling system which plants like. They also made getting the coral very difficult. When it is in the sea every little hole, sponge-like, fills with sea water which doubles the weight of the coral itself. Some of the larger ones we have took the combined efforts of both girls, the boy, Tu'ifua and myself to lift from the bottom of the sea and topple into the boat. Farquhar's part in such expeditions consisted in advising us to give them up and in treating the strained muscles and the coral cuts with which, in addition to the coral itself, we always managed to come home.

In front of the house is a wide unbroken lawn. This not only satisfied Farquhar's desire for open space, but also provided a place where the girls could set up their croquet game and where, when the villagers came down to sing and dance for us, they could perform. Around the sides and in the back, Tu'ifua and I made our coral paths and created sunny places and shady ones to provide suitable micro-climates for a great variety of growing things.

Whatever I do, I read about. Soon a shelf in the library started to fill with garden books and magazines. One article that had a great influence on us, I found in the Hawaiian magazine *Paradise of the Pacific*. It was written by Blanche Pope, who with her husband, an early agricultural officer, was responsible for many of the most beautiful hibiscus blooms for which Hawaii has become famous. Not long after I read the article, I made my first trip back to California. When I was returning to Tonga, I stopped in Hawaii and had the privilege of meeting Mrs. Pope. She was then in her mid-nineties, but like most plant people I've known had a zest for life and for her chosen work that made the years seem irrelevant. With the generosity that is also typical of plant people, she gave me seeds and cuttings of her prize plants and gave me, too, a long afternoon during which she took me into her garden and showed me how she made the crosses which had made her famous in horticultural circles.

When I got back to 'Utulei, I told Tu'ifua of my visit. We became hibiscus hybridisers and inspired a little group of local women to join us. Because it takes two months to get seed after a hibiscus is pollinated and two years from seed to blooming plant, developing new varieties requires a certain amount of patience, but it is a fascinating activity. A high percentage of the new plants will be inferior to either of the parent plants—many indeed, will be fit for nothing but the rubbish heap. Once in a hundred or so crossings, perhaps, there will be a plant whose blooms, embodying the best characteristics of both parents, seem to bring new beauty into the world. Producing one such plant is all the reward a gardener needs. When I saw the first bloom of the pure yellow hibiscus whose seed Farquhar had had exposed to X-ray, I had the heady feeling of sharing with God in the act of creation. I never now look at the bush with its dark shining leaves and its perfectly-shaped yellow blooms without feeling a return to my initial excitement.

One year there came to Vava'u an elderly American botany professor and his wife, Dr. and Mrs. Truman Yuncker. When Dr. Yuncker retired from teaching at the University of Indiana, he merely entered on a more active phase of his career. On a grant from the Bishop Museum, he came to Tonga. The flora he produced as a result of his work here has become the standard reference volume for all who want to learn of the Tongan bush. For Dr. Yuncker, no cliff was too steep to clamber down if there was a plant he wanted at its bottom and no road that promised a new variety was too long. The Yunckers stayed at the Government Rest House in Neiafu and while Dr. Yuncker was out tramping the country, Mrs. Yuncker stayed at home and cooked—not his meals, but his specimens which had to be dried slowly on a tray-like arrangement over a Primus stove. Hers was the tedious part of their work, but she performed it cheerfully and when her husband discovered a new variety of Ixora that had never before been recorded, she shared all his pride in being able to name it *Ixora yunckeri*. They came often to 'Utulei while they were in Vava'u and we learned much about the indigenous trees and shrubs from them and much, too, about the continuing sense of wonder and of joy that belongs to people who spend their lives with plants. When the Flora was published, Dr. Yuncker sent us an autographed copy. It is one of the most treasured and most used books in the house. It has helped Tu'ifua and me in our meetings with Vava'u women's groups to give the people a heightened appreciation of their native trees and shrubs and it has made it possible for us to identify the many things which we have brought home from picnics and from our walks in the bush.

Like the house, the garden has become part of our lives and like our lives, it is always changing.

CHAPTER SEVEN

A BRIEF NOTE ON MISSIONARIES

DURING MY first year in Vava'u while I was teaching at Siuilikutapu College, my immediate superior in the Wesleyan hierarchy was an Australian minister who was Chairman of the church in Vava'u. He lived across the street from the college in the big old Mission House with his wife and young son. In order to keep the three of them in the style to which, in their native Australia, they could never have become accustomed, they had four house-girls and whole squads of yardboys. Twice a week that extensive staff was augmented by a group of college girls commandeered by Mrs. Missionary to scrub the veranda, do the ironing and perform similar domestic services. None of these people was paid. " They love Jesus," the missionary explained, " and so they serve us. It is a privilege."

It was a privilege of which I very soon commenced a long battle to rid the college girls. Needless to say, my efforts in that direction did not improve my relations with the couple in the Mission House. I rarely visited them except when some college business took me over and then I was usually accompanied by Tu'ifua.

Whatever distaste they felt for me, I had still, in their eyes, the great advantage of being white. " Come in and have a cup of tea," they would say as I stood on the veranda. Then they would nod to Tu'ifua, point off to the back of the house and say, " Go and wait in the kitchen."

The first time it happened, I thought they must have some secret to tell me which they did not want her to hear. Soon, however, I became aware that it was standard mission procedure, but I could not get used to having my head tutor dismissed as if she were a scullery maid.

One day I spoke to her about it. " Don't worry," she said, " I prefer the kitchen." With a flash of the arrogance I had come to treasure, she added, " The company there is better."

As the year went on, I determined that when it was over, I would leave the college. I came to the decision, not because of my marriage, but because of the ever-widening gap between my ideas and those of church authorities. Teaching is a wonderful way to come to know people and I enjoyed the girls in my classes, but I was constantly overwhelmed by a sense of inevitable failure. Although the girls were charged what in local terms was a high tuition and were constantly being asked to make additional contributions to the church, no class had enough books to go around. Indeed, in the top English class, there were only two—one for me and one for the twenty-five girls. Nor were there any maps except for one tattered one showing the location of Wesleyan missions in the Pacific. Blackboards, paper, pencils, chalk and all similar school necessities were non-existent. Such lacks, serious though they were, might have been endured had it not been that the mission authorities regarded them with such complacency. The girls paid their school fees and they went to church regularly. That was all that was important to the missionaries.

Long after I had made up my mind to leave, I hesitated to tell Tu'ifua. When at last I did, her eyes filled with tears. " Don't go," she implored me. " I'll be so lonely here without you."

" How much do you get paid?" I asked abruptly.

" Thirty shillings a month."

" Thirty shillings," I repeated. " That's not even five dollars and for that you teach five days a week, you stay here on Saturdays until the last girl has gone home and you're back again on Saturday afternoon to see them return."

With gentle dignity, she said, " It is not for the thirty shillings I teach, but because my father has said it is my duty to the church."

" Rot," I replied. " Lots of *papalangis* work for nothing, too—but not for people who treat them the way they treat you."

Then I said to her, " When I leave, why don't you leave, too?"

" If only I could!" she said, " if only I could."

Tu'ifua's father, Fevale'aki, was an ardent churchman, but he was also an intelligent individual and a loving father. On Saturdays when she went home, Tu'ifua began to talk to him about the college and the way she and all Tongans were treated by the

(*above*) Important People: Tu'ifua, Farquhar, Tupou and Tami.
(*below*) The house at the point

Family Album: (*above left*) Tu'ifua. (*above right*) Farquhar with Tami. (*below*) Tupou and Tami on the beach

missionaries. At first he counselled her to be patient and spoke of her duty, but little by little she won him over. At last he agreed that the five years she had served as head tutor were enough to fulfill her duty.

By the year's end, I had become so outspoken a critic of missionary policy that the church authorities were relieved to see me go, but they never forgave me for taking Tu'ifua with me. After all, one does not find teachers like her very often at any price—let alone thirty shillings a month!

CHAPTER EIGHT

THE DOCTOR AND THE YOUNG MEN

The second half of the twenty years I have been in Tonga has been thronged with overseas visitors, but in the early years few people braved the tangle of air lines, steamers and small ships necessary to bring them to 'Utulei. Nevertheless, the house has always—right from the start, been full of a most cosmopolitan company, men and women and a few remarkable children, people of all races, all times, all dispositions who have given to our lives deeper meanings and heightened experiences.

There are those who would say I am only talking of characters shut up in books. In books they certainly were, but once we had opened them, their characters became our companions and a very real part of our days.

On still mornings before the early breeze had come up, when the sun was just beginning to lighten the eastern sky, I ran through the quiet garden, revelling in the new day. With me was my favourite Emily Dickinson giving words to the feelings we shared,

> Inebriate of air am I
> And debauchee of dew.

The flowers she looked on were New England blooms and the people among whom she spent her days were New Englanders, too, but her awareness and understanding are universal qualities. Often her poems have given me a fresh view of my brown-skinned neighbours or a deeper appreciation of my tropical surroundings.

After lunch, in those days, Farquhar and I used to lie down through the siesta hour—not to sleep, but to visit awhile with all the people Jane Austen brought to us or those that were given life by Thackeray. We did not rush with those people as one does with the characters of modern novels, but came to them with the slow enjoyment with which one greets old friends. While Farquhar read aloud in his deep Scotch voice, we were once again faced with the problems of the Bennetts and Mr. Knightly and Emma, once again we felt the pathos of Becky Sharpe for whom things were almost right, but always just missed being completely so, once again we were exasperated and delighted by that most complete and most lovable scoundrel, Barry Lyndon.

Down from the library shelves came explorers and adventurers, saints and sinners, beautiful women and brilliant men and a never-ending stream of simple people—all to share our days and, when the days came to an end, we watched from the veranda as the setting sun sent its last rays to tint our seas, like Homer's, wine-dark.

Among those early visitors who escaped from the library shelves were some who were not welcome. They were the ones to whom Farquhar referred scornfully as the "writing doctors". Sent by well-meaning friends who imagined he would welcome all comers of his own profession, they were men who had wandered out of practice into journalism and produced the sort of books destined to become radio or TV serials or to blossom forth as Hollywood movies. Farquhar dismissed the feats around which they built their melodramatic plots as being either impossible surgery during which any patient not provided with the cat's proverbial nine lives would certainly have succumbed or routine operations which any half-way competent doctor would have performed as easily as he would have taken a patient's temperature.

If, however, he objected to those medico-literary quacks, he had a great respect for men whose work was a genuine fusion of scientific thinking and literary skill—men like Goldsmith, Wells and Snow. But the medical man who was most often in our company in those days was a London doctor, John Martin. He has been dead now for over a century, but his mind was such a vital one, that his company is still good.

Dr. Martin must have been a perfect example of that wonderful many-sided person, a general practitioner—now, alas! in this age of specialisation, fast disappearing. With interests extending far beyond his profession, he had the same charm, the same inexhaustible curiosity about life that da Vinci and the other great men of the Renaissance exhibited. Martin himself said, " All that regards man, whether it be good or evil, is highly interesting to man."

We met the doctor through William Mariner, a young Englishman who is well known in Vava'u. They came into our house together one day when we received a second-hand copy of a small, worn leatherbound book entitled, *Mariner's Tonga by Dr. John Martin*. We had ordered the book because it is one of the few written about Vava'u and because it is an excellent source book of Tongan history. Much more than that, it was an introduction to two most amazing Englishmen.

William Mariner, the younger of the two, was born in 1791 into a family of comfortable means. At an early age, he was sent to Mr. Mitchell's Academy at Ware in Hertfordshire. When he was thirteen, Mr. Mitchell died and William returned to his home. His formal education was over. It says much for both him and the school that, according to Dr. Martin, he had then, " besides the common acquisitions of reading, writing, and arithmetic, much progress in the knowledge of history and geography and the Latin and French languages."

Mariner's father, who had sailed his own hired armed cutter in the American Revolutionary war under Lord Cornwallis, wanted William to go to sea, but, although the boy was fond of travel books and had an adventurous nature, he did not like the idea of a maritime life. When his mother backed him up, he was placed in the office of a solicitor where it was agreed that he would stay for a few months previous to articles being signed.

And so he might have done, had it not been that one night a Captain Duck who had served his apprenticeship under William's father, came to dinner. Over the meal, he told of the *Port au Prince*, a private ship of war of which he had just gained command. Those were rough days. A private ship of war was, in truth, a pirate ship, licensed by the British government to prey on the ships of her enemies. The *Port au Prince*, well furnished with cannons and miscellaneous weapons was slated to go cruising after Spanish ships, to board them and confiscate their cargoes. If she had not found sufficient prizes within a certain time and within certain latitudes, she was to sail around Cape Horn into the Pacific Ocean and search for whales. Either one of the *Port au Prince's* objectives was enough to guarantee adventure. William, listening to the man talking, felt the stirrings of old dreams. Suddenly the solicitor's office seemed to him a drab prison. He burst into conversation with the request that he be allowed to sail with Captain Duck. Old Mr. Mariner was pleased at his son's belated desire to go to sea and when Duck offered to make him his clerk, the matter was soon arranged. The *Port au Prince* sailed from Gravesend on 12th February 1805, with William on board.

Long before they ever reached the South Seas, they had had adventures enough to fill a dozen volumes. There were misadventures, too— the most significant being the death off the Mexican coast of Captain Duck. It must have come as blow to young Mariner to lose his friend and patron, particularly as the *Port au Prince* then fell into the hands of the sailing master, Mr. Brown, a man who lacked Duck's judgement in dealing both with ships and with men. Although Mariner did not like him, he apparently served him as faithfully as he had served his father's old friend.

After Captain Duck had been buried on Cedros Island, the *Port au Prince* sailed for Hawaii. There they got fresh provisions and sailed for Tahiti, but when it was discovered that they had missed it, course was set for Tonga.

By 29th November 1806 when they arrived at Ha'apai, the central island group of Tonga, the ship was leaking badly and the men were approaching a state of mutiny. They had no sooner put down the anchor than the ship was swarming with a crowd of natives. It is easy enough to condemn them as savages and to say that what they subsequently did were the brutal acts of unthinking men, but it is perhaps well to remember that the *Port au Prince* had herself attacked Spanish ships which were going peaceably about their business, had boarded them, taken prisoners—or, if they resisted, killed them—and the *Port au Prince* belonged to a nation that prided itself on being in the vanguard of civilisation. It is small wonder that the Ha'apai people who—since Europeans had sailed to their shores had come to know the value of nails and iron, regarded the *Port au Prince* as a prize sent to them by a kindly fate. Their smiles at seeing so much wealth which was soon to be theirs were interpreted by Captain Brown as simple evidences of friendship. Mariner, young though he was, knew better. He saw the weapons which the men had brought on board with them. He warned the captain, but the warning went unheeded. So certain was the master of the Tongans' friendly intentions that when two of them invited him to go ashore, he went off unarmed between them. Within minutes of reaching land, he had been clubbed to death.

Mariner, meanwhile, realising that a massacre was about to break out ran with the cooper to the magazine where they hid. When, a couple of hours later, they ventured up again, their worst fears had been realised. The place was running with blood and lined up on deck were the bodies, naked and battered, of twenty-two of their shipmates. All about natives with their bloody clubs still in their hands were busy pillaging the cabins and cargo.

It is not surprising that Mariner, who was only fifteen at the time, felt so great a shock that the events of the next few days passed as if they were happening in a dream. Fortunately for him, he had been noticed by Finau, the great chief of Ha'apai and Vava'u, who had given the order that, in the general massacre, he was to be saved. He was taken ashore where he was very rudely treated by the common people who tore off his clothes, threw rocks at him and spat at him, but as soon as he reached Finau's enclosure, he was received kindly. There he was bathed, his skin was rubbed with scented coconut oil, he was presented with robes made of new *tapa* cloth. He was given the name " Toku'ukumea," of a recently deceased son of the chief.

In those days when ships that had made successful voyages into the Pacific were homeward bound to England or France or America, they most often carried on board a South Sea Islander to exhibit in the salons and drawing rooms of London, Paris, or New York. Curiosity being among the human traits that is not limited by colour, it is not surprising that in the islands, native chiefs vied with one another to see who could keep the most interesting white men. There is no doubt that Mariner, who was a most handsome youth, was, at first, regarded by Finau merely as a pet *papalangi*, but both men had a great capacity for loyalty and friendship and before long their relationship was that of father and son.

For four years Mariner lived in Tonga—most of the time in Vava'u which was Finau's home, but for this country those were tumultuous times of civil wars. Finau was in the thick of them and Mariner with him—now in Ha'apai, now in Tongatapu. In between battles, they came back to Vava'u where they lived the idyllic life that people like to think always goes on in the islands—fishing and swimming, singing and hunting and feasting. In everything that went on around him, Mariner was interested. He learned to speak the language so well that in the dark of night he was often mistaken by the natives for one of their own number. He mastered the involved political situation and knew as much of intrigue as any courtier who ever lived. When Finau died and was succeeded by his son, he established with the younger Finau the same close relationship he had enjoyed with his father. The extent of their understanding may be judged by the fact that when at last the *Favourite*, a British ship bound for the East Indies, sailed into Vava'u, Finau freely gave his consent to Mariner to go off in her because he realised " his father must be anxious about him."

By the time Mariner arrived back in England, he was twenty years old, but he had had more adventures than befall most men in their whole lives. Only three years his senior, John Martin had also had adventures, but his were those of the human mind and spirit. Already an established doctor in London, he had studied meteorology and produced meteorological charts. An avid reader, he had been fired by all the adventurous books that were written about the new world that was opening up in the Pacific. His imagination, however, was tempered by the scientific approach. He regarded the South Sea Islanders, not as strange brown men with savage ways and strange customs, but as fellow members of the human race. The term "anthropologist" had not come into use in his day, but he was a true one. He said, " The infancy of human society in our times probably differs not much, except in local circumstances, from that which existed four thousand years ago: by a scrupulous and attentive examination of the present, therefore, we may be able to form some tolerable judgement of the past."

He had been longing to be able to make a detailed study of some primitive peoples when in 1811 he formed, as he says, " an accidental acquaintance with Mr. William Mariner, recently arrived from the East Indies, the bearer of a letter to one of my connections in London. Hearing that he had been a resident among the natives of the Tongan Islands, during a space of four years, my curiosity was much excited."

There must have been many meetings after the initial one. Soon Dr. Martin had heard all Mariner had to tell of his stay in

Tonga. He felt that because Mariner had been so young at the time he arrived in Tonga, he had accepted what he saw without trying, as most white men would have done, to judge it. The doctor's scientific mind was delighted by the fact that Mariner had "no disposition to over-rate or embellish what to him was neither strange nor new."

Very soon he was urging his young friend to write down all he had told him, but Mariner said he could not. For so long had he been unused to writing or even reading that the labour of finding words for his adventures seemed impossible.

Mariner's refusal to write his Tongan memoirs was fortunate. It sparked off one of the most unusual and most successful of all literary collaborations. Martin volunteered to write the book if Mariner would supply the material. As a first step, he suggested that Mariner, who was about to make a trip to the West Indies, write down in chronological order everything he remembered about Tonga.

The plan, as sketched by the doctor, is simple and thorough. He said, "It was ultimately determined that I should undertake the composition and arrangement of the intended work, while Mr. Mariner should direct his attention to the materials; noting down all that he had seen and heard, as such occurred to his mind. These materials were afterwards made subjects of conversation and strict scrutiny; and not one of the ensuing pages has been written without his presence and approval."

When Mariner came back from the West Indies, it was at once apparent that he had done his homework well. He brought back sheaves of notes. Farquhar and I used to talk of those conversations the two men had about Tonga. What wonderful ones they would have been to listen-in on! The almost total recall exhibited by Mariner is remarkable and no less so is Martin's ability to comprehend and make his own the experience of another. The book that they produced is a little masterpiece. Not only does it describe with complete accuracy the political situation of the time, it gives also what remains today the best guide to old-time Tongan customs and beliefs and it is invaluable for anyone who wishes to understand the Tongan mind.

Taken alone, Mariner's Tonga is a great work, but it has also appendices that make it even more valuable. Mariner wrote out a vocabulary of between 400 and 600 Tongan words and gave it to

Dr. Martin. The two men went over each word, Mariner pronouncing it carefully and Dr. Martin writing it down. Martin, however, was not satisfied. He gave Mariner an English dictionary and had him go through it putting Tongan equivalents to every word he could. Then he had him write down all he could remember of speeches he had heard and bits of conversation. In the end, he had a vocabulary of over 8,000 words. Working from it, he deduced the principles of the language and wrote an excellent grammar.

In Dr. Martin's day, every man who set out to write down the Polynesian languages wrote the words as he heard them. Martin's orthography is, in many instances, not that used today. He wrote, for example, a "g" where modern Tongan spelling demands a "k". His ear was more acute than that of the early missionary who wrote "k" for the "g" sound persists in modern spoken Tongan. Tongans even carry it over into English so that we are all delighted by the radio announcer who tells us nightly about the weather on the "ghost".

Unfortunately most of the *papalangis* who live in Tonga nowadays are gifted neither with Martin's linguistic ability nor with Mariner's photographic memory. The Tongan language is a difficult one. All of us who try to speak it have a humiliating list of 'boners' to our credit. I think that in my twenty years in Tonga, there has been only one white man here who belongs in the class of Mariner and Martin. He is Eric Schumway, a young Mormon who did his missionary work here in Vava'u. Six months the Mormon church gives its young men to learn the language. Most of them at the end of that time, can get along creditably if not fluently. Schumway, however, combining Mariner's gift of total recall with Martin's linguistic ability, spoke as an educated Tongan who loves his native tongue. When he had completed his mission time, he went to the Church College of the Pacific at Laie, Hawaii, where he worked in the Department of Languages. There he wrote the Tongan grammar and language book which has become the standard text studied by all volunteers to the Tongan Peace Corps programme during their training in Hawaii. It is the first book that makes Tongan a possible language for ordinary students.

But to get back to Mariner's book—in addition to the grammar and vocabulary, there is a section based on his observations and conversations with the natives which deals with the surgical skill of the Tongans. It was, for those days, considerable, and I may note here that today Tongans, a manually dextrous people, still make excellent surgeons.

Interesting people attract other interesting people. Martin seems to have had accomplished friends in many fields. One of them was a musician. Martin enlisted his help when he came to write the section on Tongan music. Mariner sang for them all the songs he could remember. Martin's friend wrote them down and from them he came to a very just view of Tongan music. The section has been of value to modern Tongans because it contains many old songs and much old dance music which, had it not been recorded by Mariner might well have been lost by now.

To some people it may seem that William Mariner and Dr. John Martin are shut up in the two worn volumes on our library shelves, but to us they are real and welcome visitors. It is good to have such friends who share our interest in Tonga's people and who appreciate her natural beauty.

CHAPTER NINE

VE'EMUMUNI

TONGANS ARE not given to dotting their land with brass markers to explain where important events took place. Consequently the casual one-day tourists go away as often as not without, as they say, "Having seen anything". Actually these islands are full of significant places marked by that most durable of all things—the memory of man.

When you have been here a while, you begin to hear the stories attached to the places round about and story and place grow together in your mind to form an integral whole. Often we go over to the main island to the reef below the village of Tola to look for the black snake-head cowrie shells that we find at low tide in the crevices of the coral. When we are there, after we have found our shells and are hot from the sunny reef, we climb up the steep trail that rises from the beach to the pool of Ve'emumuni which lies in a cave, the entrance to which is almost hidden by a fold of rock that hangs half-way up the cliff. As the water there is always cool and fresh even on the hottest days, the pool is a favourite swimming place. In time of drought, it gives the Tola people water for their households and for their gardens. These days Ve'emumuni belongs to all men alike, but it was not always so.

Once it belonged to a beautiful being who guarded it jealously and kept its waters to herself. She sealed the entrance with a heavy stone, but every now and then, she would lift the stone and sit on it and watch a man who was working in his garden nearby.

One day, the man looked up and saw her and, marvelling at her beauty, drew near to speak to her; but, before he could reach her, she had disappeared into the pool and drawn the stone after her. He went back to work and when he looked up again, there she was, beautiful, smiling, faintly mocking. Again he approached her and again she disappeared. When this had happened three times, he understood that she was not a mortal woman, but a spirit.

The man took off his turban and removed the girdle of leaves he was wearing and draped them over a tree so that they resembled a man standing in the middle of his garden. He crouched low in the bushes and saw that the spirit was indeed deceived into thinking the tree was himself. Then, stepping very cautiously so that no twig would break beneath his foot and no bird start up at his approach, he crept around behind the spirit.

Suddenly he leapt at her and held her tight in both hands. She struggled and tried to get away, but the man was young and strong and she could not get free. Finally, she begged for mercy and told him she would give him the pool if he would let her go. He released her and she was never seen again and the man had the pool. He threw away the rock that had covered the entrance and from that day to this Ve'emumuni's waters have been free to all men.

CHAPTER TEN

A PICNIC AND TALAFAIVA

HOT DOGS and Tu'ifua's home-made rolls, bottles of lemonade and a thermos of tea, a chocolate cake with thick frosting and the biggest watermelon the market offered were put in the boat with rolled up mats and baskets full of bathing suits and snorkelling equipment, with extra benzine for the engine and a pair of oars in case the engine gave out.

Then Nia who lives up the hill from us here in 'Utulei, Kay, Peter and Ursula—visiting friends, and I squeezed in, too, and we floated at anchor waiting for Tu'ifua. Every now and then, with my usual impatience, I shouted up at the house saying, "*Ha'u Fua, vave!*"—Come, Fua, quickly. As usual, my shouting produced no results. I fussed about the hours I had spent waiting for her and gave up and talked of other things. After what seemed a great length of time, she appeared at the top of the path. Her hands were filled with the oarlocks, a can opener, an extra mat and a big plastic bottle of water, but she came towards us regally, advancing as slowly as if time did not exist.

"At last," I said as she climbed into the boat.

She made a scornful remark about people who rushed about and left her to gather up the things they had forgotten, pulled up the anchor and smiled at our friends. I started the engine, the sun peeped out from a sheltering cloud and we were off down the harbour.

In a few moments we had left 'Utulei behind and approached the little round island of Lotuma which people hereabouts say used to be the top of Talau, the mountain opposite our house. It was stolen one day by a Samoan devil who would have carried it home with him had not a clever Tongan spirit tickled him and forced him to drop it just off the end of our island.

I could see Tu'ifua telling the story to Peter and Ursula and

Nia repeating it to Kay. As for me, I was content to listen to the whirr of the engine, look at the deep blue water and watch the islands that lay on either side of the long channel down which we were going. Past the neighbouring village of 'Utugake with its wide sandy beach, we went and across the pass where tiny Mala and its rocky islet, a Tongan Scylla and Charybodis, is all that stands between us and the open sea. A rough stretch that was, with the waves lapping over the side of the boat every few minutes, but the sea calmed as we came into the lee of the next island, Kapa.

"Shall we go into the Cave?" I called and Tu'ifua nodded, "Of course," so I steered the boat close up under the island's rocky end, turned the corner, and went into the cliff through a narrow passage that led to the watery chamber that is the famous Swallow's Cave. When we were inside, I cut the engine and we drifted in silence in the cathedral-like room that is almost 100 feet high and 200 in circumference and whose limestone walls, in the light that comes in through the opening passage, glow with as many colours as a stained-glass window. Then, a chirr and a whirr and a host of birds (which, my bird-watching friends tell me, are not swallows at all, but swifts) flew in excited swoops above us and about the cave, out through the opening and back again. From high on the ceiling, we could see their nests built of mud, looking like suspended apartment houses.

"Even here," Kay said, "people find it necessary to scribble their names on the walls."

Unfortunately it is true, but such is the power of time, that even while we deplored the late comers who had splashed their names in white paint, we found a certain interest in paddling over to the far dark side of the cave and reading there the names of whalers and other roving seamen who had visited the place early in the last century.

"It's seventy fathoms deep," Tu'ifua said in answer to a question from Peter and he and Ursula got out their cameras and tried to capture on film the cerulean shine of the clear water that is the floor of the cave.

We made a final circuit, pausing at the bell rock which Tu'ifua pounded with an oar so we could hear its solemn knell. Then I started the engine and once more we were outside in the sunlit island-studied world.

On our left, on Kapa island, we passed the crescent Port Maurelle, named for the Spaniard who was the first European to see Vava'u and soon to the right we saw Nuku, the jewel-like island on whose white sand beaches so many generations of both Tongans and *papalangis* have picnicked.

Usually we stop there at Nuku, but on this day we had a more distant objective—the island of Euakafa. South we went and west over a stretch of open sea that tossed our little boat and splashed us. Before long, we were wet through and through, but the day was warm and we were in holiday mood; so, we laughed and licked the salt from our lips.

"That island keeps moving away," Kay said and it seemed her words were true. What from Nuku had looked like a short, easy run stretched out and out as we ploughed through the sea, but at last the waves grew less wild and, at the base of Euakafa's wooded slopes, we saw a long curve of white beach. A few minutes more and we were pulling the boat on to the sand and carrying our picnic things up to a grassy place where a grove of cassia trees cast their sun-dappled shade.

Peter gathered wood for a fire. The hot dogs were grilled and, in amazing quantity in an amazingly short time, eaten. When we had had our fill of them and of all the other good things we had brought, we lay back on the mats—sometimes talking, sometimes singing, sometimes merely staring out to sea. Our postprandial content was interrupted by Tu'ifua who said abruptly, "We'd better go to the tomb now."

The tomb which was what we had come all that distance to see belongs to Talafaiva, an old Tongan queen and it is on the very summit of Euakafa, a height which the chart says is 270 feet. When you say it, 270 feet is nothing at all, but I had been to the top before and I knew the steep path that rises up the rocky cliff face, the thicket-like branches that tear clothes and scratch faces, the roots that give way when you grab them.

"Let's wait awhile," I sat lazily.

Tu'ifua would probably have turned a deaf ear to my request had not Nia helped. "You'd better tell us about Talafaiva before we go to look at her tomb," she said. When Peter and Ursula and Kay agreed, Tu'ifua settled back with a sigh.

"Well then," she began, "long ago—maybe in the seventeenth century—there was a King of Tonga called Telea. He had three or four wives, but each of them had brought him fifty or sixty women besides so he really had over a hundred..."

"Whew!" broke in Peter, "Those were the days!"

Tu'ifua frowned and said primly, "He loved one of his wives better than all the others. Her name was Talafaiva. She was young and beautiful and when Telea was by her side he forgot all the rest of the world.

"He brought her here to this island of Euakafa and had a beautiful house built for her high on the top of the mountain. Around it were wide grounds enclosed by a woven reed fence. Talafaiva was delighted with her new home, but when she came to inspect the grounds, she saw, growing close to the fence a *fo'ui tree*, whose branches stretched far over into the bush land beyond the enclosure.

"'Please have that tree cut down,' she said to Telea. 'It is too close to the fence. Someone could climb up it and come in and harm us'."

Tu'ifua stopped, looked at Peter, the only man in our group and said indulgently, "Men always think they know best." Then she went on with her story. "Telea just laughed at her suggestion and forgot all about it."

"For a long time they lived in their beautiful house and were very happy, but one day Lolomanaia came from his home in Makave on the main island to stay at Euakafa."

"And who was he?" Ursula asked.

"He was," said Tu'ifua simply, "one of Vava'u's handsome men."

"What did he do?" Kay demanded.

Tu'ifua frowned at what she obviously considered an irrelevant question. "He came from a chiefly family—and mostly he just ran off with girls."

"Nice occupation," murmured Peter as Tu'ifua went on to explain, "He had heard of Talafaiva, of her beauty and her grace and her sweet disposition, so he came here to Euakafa to see her for himself. And as soon as he saw her, he fell in love with her."

"It wasn't long before a night came when Telea decided to go fishing in the deep waters beyond the reef. Lolomanaia had been waiting for just such a chance. As soon as it was dark, he went up to the reed fence and tried to push the gate open, but it was firmly locked and guards stood just behind it. Dejectedly he

(*above*) Back to the house. (*below*) The Mathesons

(*above*) Sunset view of Vava'u harbour from Neiafu. 'Utulei village is behind the point on the left. (*below*) The house

walked around the fence looking for some hole in it, but there was none. Then he spotted the *fo'ui* tree. He lost no time in grasping a low branch and climbing up and in a very few minutes, he was on the other side of the fence, inside the royal enclosure and on his way to Talafaiva."

Like all Vava'uans, Tu'ifua has a weakness for the old time legendary handsome men. " You must understand," she said, looking round at us, " that no one could resist Lolomanaia. He was so very handsome. So, even though Talafaiva was a good wife and loved her husband, she listened to Lolomanaia and all that night he was with her. When he was leaving her at day break, he made a mark on her belly which was the sign he always left on the women he slept with . . ."

" He was a kiss and tell," I said, but Tu'ifua ignored the remark and went on, " The next day, Telea came home and he went in to sleep with Talafaiva, but when he saw Lolomanaia's mark on her, he knew what had happened and he flew into a great rage.

" Talafaiva tearfully begged his pardon, explaining that she had been overpowered by Lolomanaia's charms, but her irate husband would not listen to her. He ranted and raved until at last her patience gave out and she turned on him. 'Telea', she said, 'you remember I asked you to cut down the *fo'ui* tree and you would not do it. It was not I who let Lolomanaia in. It was your *fo'ui*.'

" When she said that, Telea's wrath grew so great that he called Uka, his manservant, and pointing to Talafaiva said, 'Take her and beat her' and turning his back on them, he plunged down the hillside to the beach where he walked up and down until his rage subsided.

" He walked back up the hill at last and going into the enclosure called Uka. 'Have you beaten her?' he asked and the servant said, 'I have beaten her'.

When Telea heard that, his heart softened toward his beautiful wife. Filled with concern, he asked, 'And how is she?'

" 'She is dead,' Uka said.

" 'Is she quite dead?' Telea asked.

" 'She is quite dead.'

" 'My wife, Talafaiva, is she quite dead?'

" 'She is quite dead.'

" Then Telea was grief-stricken and he cried out to Uka, 'I did not want you to kill her. I only meant for you to beat her a little because I was angry. I loved her and you have killed her! You are an old fool.' And he went and wept over Talafaiva for a day and a night. And he built the great stone tomb that is on the top of the mountain and she was buried there."

Half an hour later, after a steep climb that had us all out of breath, we reached the top of Euakafa and came to a wide raised rectangle faced with dressed coral rock. Once the surface was cleared and grassy, but over the centuries since Telea built it, a thick tangle of trees and shrubs has grown over it. We pushed our way through them until we came to an open place where a shaft of sunlight fell on a moss-covered coral slab that had cracked to show beneath it a deep rock-walled vault.

"Here it is," Tu'ifua announced. "Talafaiva's tomb."

"But where's Talafaiva?" Kay asked peering into the empty tomb on whose green sides ferns had begun to grow.

Tu'ifua shook her head. "No one knows. Maybe somebody stole her body and buried it somewhere else. Maybe Lolomanaia did. Maybe Telea never really buried her here at all, but found a secret place for her. No one knows, but this is Talafaiva's tomb."

We lingered awhile in the sad spot, listening to a bird singing from the top of a nearby tree and then we crossed over to the far side of the mountain where we could see still the stones that had marked out the dwelling houses in the enclosure where Telea and Talafaiva had lived, but the reed fence was gone and gone, too, was the cause of the tragedy—the *fo'ui* tree.

Later, after our swimming and snorkelling, after all our explorations of reef and bush, after tea, when we were all in the boat with the plants and shells and the driftwood that were our souvenirs of the day, we went back up through the islands. The sea had gone down, the world was tinged with sunset purple.

"*Fo'ui ne fai*," said Tu'ifua, "It's become a Tongan proverb . . . the *fo'ui* did it." We laughed at the age-old urge to blame someone or something else for one's own weaknesses, but our laughter died away as we thought again of the empty tomb high on the hill.

Then Tu'ifua and Nia began to sing an old love song. Soon the others joined in. They sang all the way back home to 'Utulei.

CHAPTER ELEVEN

THE STORY-TELLING WEAVER

A UNIVERSITY professor of mine used to say that the trouble with communism was that, like Christianity, it had never been tried. I suspect that—with the exception of a few outstanding individual cases, he was right about Christianity, but about communism, he was wrong. The daily life of pre-European Polynesians was thoroughly communal. Group-work and group sharing were the rule. Today in Tonga much of that old feeling survives. Nowhere is it more in evidence than in the women's working committees which flourish all over the country.

Tu'ifua belongs to one such committee that specialises in weaving. Ten women meet one day a week, each week in the house of a different woman. The hostess for the day provides lunch and a place to work. All day long the members of the committee weave on a mat for the hostess. Once the pandanus leaves have been cut and prepared, ten women working together can finish quite a large mat in one day.

When Tu'ifua first told me about the committee, I asked her how she could possibly belong to it. It is true that she knows all the old traditional patterns and has the basic good taste to enable her to evaluate new ones. She has, moreover, a thorough knowledge of all the different plants which can be used both for the fibre itself and for colouring it. However, the undeniable fact remains that in spite of her wisdom about mats, she is a most indifferent weaver.

Knowing that, I repeated, "What good are you to a weaving committee."

Rather huffily, she replied, "As a matter of fact, I'm very important to my committee. If it wasn't for me, they wouldn't get half as much weaving done."

I laughed scornfully, but she went on, " I tell them stories."

For months, whenever she was in 'Utulei with us, she had been buried in the *Mutiny on the Bounty*. I learned then that each week she told the weavers what she had read the preceding weekend. Half an hour would be more than ample for me to tell the story that Nordhoff and Hall wrote, but Tongans would be bored by the mere outline of events that I would give. They want to know how each character looked, what he wore, when he got up in the morning, what he did during the day, which people he met and what plants and animals he saw. Catering to their love of detail and allowing frequent pauses during which the women could ask questions and gossip about the people in the book just as they gossip about the people in the village, Tu'ifua was able to spin the story out for months.

Her favourite books for such telling were those that dealt with Polynesia for Tongans have a lively interest in their own culture and background, but detective stories got much weaving done and I have seen a beautifully patterned mat that was woven to the tragic tale that Maupassant tells of "The Necklace".

CHAPTER TWELVE

'UTULEI BEACH SCHOOL

WELL BEFORE her first birthday, Tami learned to walk. That ability led us both into four enchanted years. Beyond our own big garden, lay the village and beyond that, the bush lands with the food plots of the 'Utulei people. Even further away were the wild places—dark forests where grew the great trees that bear the almond-like *ai* nuts, the *ifi* or Polynesian chestnut and the *tava*, a delicate fruit with the consistency of jelly. At our own front door lay the road to more distant adventure—the sea. I had a bright yellow outrigger canoe in which we could paddle across the harbour to other islands or float for long hours over the reef.

Soon Tupou was part of all our days and all our explorations. Both she and Tami were sturdy young things whose excellent health gave them a sharpened set of perceptions. Every day they learned something new about their world—the name of a plant, the call of the shy *sikiviu*, the black and white sparrow-like bird whose song begins our days, the way the Southern cross moves across the dark sky. They acquired new skills, too, learning how to keep their balance in a canoe, experiencing the joy of swimming in the velvety warm sea, singing the haunting Tongan lullabies, juggling a fistful of hard round passion fruit.

When I suggested to Farquhar that we should send away for a kindergarten course for them, he laughed at me.

" Don't be silly," he said. " 'Utulei is the best kindergarten that any child ever had."

I had been reading Montessori and spoke of the aesthetic training her kindergarten gave. He agreed that she had been a brilliant educator, but said, " That's all very well for children who live in city apartments with parents who are too busy to watch over them or answer their questions, but our girls don't need that."

When I was still unconvinced, he took me out to the front veranda. It is made of Tongan timber and is full of knot holes, but it was a gala veranda that day. Tami and Tupou had picked every hibiscus that was within their reach and, bringing the blooms to the top of the steps, had sorted them out according to the most subtle gradations of colour. Then they had stuck them into knot-holes all up the length of the veranda so that, starting at the top of the steps with a pure white bloom, you could travel to the very end, advancing from delicate pink to a deep flaming scarlet. Pointing to the display, Farquhar asked, " What would you gain by penning them up every day and having them learn about colour by matching swatches of wool?"

It was not hard to admit he was right. These islands are, indeed, a gentle nursery in which one can wander through all the long days of childhood without ever coming to harm. There are no wild animals here and no snakes twist through the thick green grass. The village women are never too busy to show a child how to plait a ring of pandanus fibre or how to start a tiny mat. The men at work in the bush gardens will always stop to tell an inquiring child the name of a plant, to point out the shortest way home to one who is lost, or to climb after a drinking nut for a thirsty one.

The land provides security. The sea teaches all one needs to know of danger. Very early the girls learned, as all village children do, to wade down the gradually-shelving beach until they were almost beyond their depth and then to turn and dive toward the shore. It was only after they had become accomplished divers that they learned to swim. Then their lives became truly amphibious and they played in the sea as much as they played on land, but they learned that there are things there to fear. They saw the quick flash of the eel whose bite can cause a painful wound and, from the safety of the boat, glimpsed the big black-and-yellow-banded sea serpent whose look is evil and whose bite is fatal. One afternoon they heard the anguished sobs of a woman who had stepped on a stonefish and they knew the long, double-edged sword of the sting ray's tail. Often they had listened while the villagers told of a fishing trip from which a whole boatload of 'Utulei's strongest young men never returned.

The knowledge of such dangers, coming to them early and naturally filled them—not with unreasoning fears, but with a very sensible feeling of caution. They revelled in the sea, learning to swim and paddle a canoe and row a boat—learning, too how to find shellfish in the crevices of the reef, but they displayed none of that dangerous *braggadocio* so often exhibited by city children when they get into the water.

Farquhar had made sure those paradisical days would last as long as possible, but eventually there came a time when school was a question that could no longer be put off. There was never any thought of sending Tami to the village school. It was held in those days in a broken down old Tongan building. The children sat on the sand floor and bent over to write on boards they held on their knees. There were neither blackboards, nor books, nor maps. The teacher whose sole preparation for his job was a dislike of going with the other men to the bush to work in the gardens was both physically and mentally the laziest Tongan I have encountered. It is small wonder that the mentally alert infants who had the misfortune to fall under his tutelage developed in a few years into muddle-headed children to whom the three Rs were a complete mystery. There were better schools elsewhere in Vava'u, but none of them offered a real education in any sense of the word and all were geared to Tongan-speaking children. Usually ex-patriates send their children overseas to school, but we both felt that there were still many things which Tami could best learn from her home. The only solutions to our problem was for me to teach her with the aid of correspondence lessons.

Just before Tami's fifth birthday, I took her to America to see her grandparents and while we were there I investigated correspondence schools and chose what I thought was the best one for our purpose. When we returned to 'Utulei—although we had been gone only four months, Tami had not only forgotten how to speak Tongan, but had forgotten even that such a language existed. As she had always played in Tongan, she was a forlorn little creature as she discovered that neither Tupou nor the other children had the vaguest idea what the English words she said to them meant. To be sure, it was not more than a fortnight before she had the language back again, but in that fortnight, I decided that I could not teach Tupou, too. I felt so uncertain of my abilities as a teacher that taking on a Tongan speaking child seemed impossible. I did not, however, want Tupou to go to our poor village school, so I asked Sister Annuncia, the American nun at the convent in Neifau, if they would take her there. She agreed and that year Tami and Tupou both started school ... Tupou at the convent and Tami at home with me.

For Tami and me those first school days were tempestuous. I have a painful memory of one sunny morning when we were having school on our side veranda. My tiny daughter stood before me, her long yellow braids glinting in the sunlight.

We had spent days together counting flowers and shells, counting knives and forks, counting crayons and bits of chalk and now I said, " Count from one to ten."

Obediently she began, " One, two three ..." and a boat passed on its way up the harbour.

" Tami," I thundered, " Never mind the boat. Count."

" Three ... three ... six?" she guessed.

" No."

" Five?"

" No, no, no," I shouted. " Have you no sense at all? One, two, three, four, five, six, seven, eight, nine, ten. Do you hear?"

She choked back a sob. " Yes, I hear."

" Repeat it then."

" One, two three, three, three ..." and down the harbour came the familiar sound of Farquhar's engine. He was coming back from the hospital early. At the sound, Tami fled off the veranda and, running to the beach to meet him, clasped her arms about his legs, and burying her head, sobbed against him.

I have talked to many people who have taught their own children—some of them experienced teachers, and all have similar confessions to make. The way one reacts to children in general has nothing at all to do with the way one reacts to one's own. During my year at the college, I had never had trouble with my students. In 'Utulei, I had taken village children for English lessons and our classes always proceeded in perfect harmony. Perhaps because I knew how poor their previous teaching had been and how scant a background for study they had, I expected little from them and found it easy to be patient.

My impatience with Tami made us all unhappy. Frankly, it puzzled me. I have since come to understand that when one teaches one's own child, all one's latent vanity is aroused. Through the distorting mirror of time, one looks back on one's own childhood. There one sees not the imperfect little being, stumbling from one mistake to another, that one really was, but a remarkable prodigy with the body of a child and one's own adult mind. It is to that wonderful, but never existent being that one compares one's child. The inevitable result is disaster.

Fortunately for Tami, she had two parents. If one was impatient to the point of being irrational, the other was always understanding. During some years that he had spent in New Zealand, Farquhar had had a private hospital, specialising in the care of babies and children. The knowledge he gained there, plus his innate gentleness, gave him a rare ability to deal with children and to handle their problems. "The trouble with you," he said to me after one stormy school session, "is that you expect Tami to act like a university student. You forget she's just a little girl."

He talked to me then of all that a small child has to learn—quite aside from school lessons, of sights and sounds and tastes and feelings. He spoke of his own childhood and led me back to mine, making me discover for myself the child I had really been in place of the one I had liked to imagine I was. Little by little I began to have a better understanding of the world as it looks to a five-year-old. Gradually I came to a more relaxed approach to school, gradually I began to regard Tami, not as an extension of myself, but as a brand new individual who would discover the world in her own way at her own tempo.

Farquhar's sister, Meg, gave many years of her life to teaching retarded children in the slums of Glasgow. She wrote him once of the joy she felt when one particularly backward child, after a year of arithmetic, was able to say with complete assurance that two and two made four. I admired her greatly, but I could never have followed her. Had I been faced with a stupid child, I would have failed completely. Fortunately for all concerned, Tami's brain was a perfectly healthy workable one. Once I got her teacher under control, she made rapid progress. Soon the morning hours during which we worked at lessons became happy times for us both. Then, instead of meeting Farquhar and sobbing against him, she ran proudly to tell him of the new things she had learned.

One year passed and two and the routine of school was firmly established. Tami continued to do well, but I began to be aware that she was no longer the happy child she had been. So long as we were at lessons, she was content, but in the afternoons, I would find her at the foot of the garden staring disconsolately up the harbour. "What are you doing?" I would ask and "Waiting for Tupou to come home," she would reply.

Convent classes finished at one o'clock. As it only takes ten or fifteen minutes to cross the harbour, it had seemed that Tami and Tupou would have all their afternoons free to play together. It did not work out that way. Mornings Tupou got across to school easily enough, going over with the village men who worked in Neiafu, but after school, she rarely found a boat coming down the harbour. Most often she had to wait around town until five o'clock when the working men were ready to come home. By the time she reached 'Utulei, it was growing dark and there was nothing left of the afternoon. Both she and Tami missed the companionship that they had so long enjoyed. What was even worse, the strain of hanging about town and the meals she all too often missed had begun to tell on Tupou physically. She grew thin and her hair developed that unnatural silkiness that is a sign of malnutrition. I was worried about her and about Tami, too.

By that time I had worked through the worst of my faults as a teacher and had vastly more confidence in my general ability to impart knowledge. I began to think that, since Tami was getting along so well, I might tackle Tupou.

One day when I found Tami staring down the harbour, I said to her, "How would you like to have Tupou come to school with us next term?"

She shouted with glee and when, a few minutes later, Tupou arrived on the beach, ran to tell her. They were both so excited that they insisted I go at once that very day to talk to Soko and Felemi, Tupou's parents.

By not having Tupou come to school with us from the very beginning, I had made myself a lot of trouble. Organised as it was for Tongan-speaking children, the convent had done little to further her knowledge of English. When the third grade started, I had virtually two classes. While Tami worked on her own, I sat with Tupou going over and over English words and simple sentences. At meals, whenever Farquhar or I spoke to her, Tupou would give us a startled look, turn to Tami and ask in rapidly whispered Tongan, "What are they saying? What do they want?"

My natural impatience began to show itself again. I wanted Tupou to learn English and to learn it quickly. After the first week of school, I said to her, "Come and stay with us for a month.

It will help your English." It did that and, as I have said elsewhere, it did more than that; for the month never ended. It gave us our second daughter.

By the time we started the fourth grade, Tupou's English was as good as Tami's. In intelligence and interest, the girls were well enough matched to provide all through the coming years stimulation and competition for one another.

'Utulei Beach School, as we called our two-pupil institution, was not entirely a one-teacher school. From the beginning Tu'ifua gave the girls weekly lessons in the Tongan language and in Tongan history and customs. She taught them singing too, as I, who could never carry a tune, was incapable of doing.

Other lacks of mine were supplied by the convent. Sister Priscilla taught the girls how to sew and, under the guidance of Sister Nicholas, they learned how to knit and made Farquhar a warm sweater that he treasured. Fortunately, there have always been French-speaking nuns at the convent. The young Sister Fabienne who comes from Vermont started them on French. When they reached high school, I did grammar with them all week and on Saturdays, Sister Albina gave them conversation and told them stories of her native Brittany. It is one of the triumphs of U.B.S. and the nuns that the girls came to share with Farquhar and me an interest in French language and literature and yet escaped from having the atrocious French pronounciation of either of us.

Tongan crafts, so much a part of most local schools, had a place in our curriculum, too. Soko, Tupou's mother, taught them how to prepare pandanus leaves for weaving and showed them how to make simple mats and baskets.

We never had gym classes—partly because I had hated the subject so much in my own school days, but even more because an hour devoted to formal exercises seemed completely unnecessary for girls who swam every day and led such a healthy outdoor life as Tami and Tupou did. They did have Tongan-dancing instructions along with a dozen or so other girls their own age, but that was so much fun they never thought of it as a class.

'Utulei Beach School boasted a few modern teaching aids, but one that was of great use was our little transistor gramophone. Each year we bought a new set of the graded series of classical records that a Californian friend had recommended. The half-hour of music gave us all a welcome break in the morning and introduced the girls to some of the great works of Western composers. Later records helped fix their French and Latin pronunciations. About the same time, we began to collect sets of Shakespeare plays. These enlivened English classes and gave us all many hours of enjoyment.

One thing that 'Utulei Beach School had in far greater abundance than any other Vava'u school, was books. I dislike the way modern textbooks dismember literature, giving a few verses of this poem and a few of another, a scene or two from a famous play, a sketch from a great novel. Fortunately we had not only books, but time; so I taught the girls to read complete poems and whole books—to savour all an author's work instead of a snippet here and a snippet there. That was one lesson they learned eagerly. I think their continuing love of books is one of the successes of the school.

'Utulei Beach School outlived its stormy beginning to become a very good school. I could write much more of it, but perhaps everything I might say could be summed up by noting that in it, as in all really good schools, the teacher learned as much as the pupils.

CHAPTER THIRTEEN

THE TURTLE

"Would you like a turtle?" Farquhar asked me one day when he came home from the hospital.

" I don't know," I said. " Would you?"

He smiled. " Probably not, but it might be interesting for the girls to watch it grow. Siketi, the driver of the government launch, found a nest of little ones just hatching out on one of the outer islands."

Tami and Tupou who had come up while we had been talking settled the question. We would have a turtle. Next day I went to Neiafu with Farquhar, carrying with me the top of my double boiler. We tied the boat up at the Rest House wharf and walked to the little house at the wharf's end where Siketi lived. When he saw us, he came running out and led us to a big copper that stood under a tree in the yard.

" Here they are," he said and we looked down and saw fifty or so coin-sized turtles swimming merrily about.

" Pick out the one you want," he said. As they were all, to our eyes exactly alike, there was no problem about choosing. We scooped up the first one we could catch and put him into the double boiler which I had already filled with sea water.

" Wait a minute," Siketi said when we thanked him and started to go. " You've got two girls now, so you'd better have two turtles."

And so it happened that we came across the harbour with our two new pets in the top of the double boiler. A washbasin which we put on the side verandah made an ideal home for them.

" What do they eat?" Tami asked.

" Siketi says they most like shell fish that you can get from the reef."

"That will be easy," Tupou said.

"And their water must be changed every day," I added.

"That will be easy, too," said the optimistic Tupou.

It was easy at first, but turtles, in common with other living things, grow. It was not long before, on still nights, I would hear them splashing about in the basin. Fearing they had come to some nameless trouble, I would get out of bed and go out to see if they were all right. As I invariably knocked against something on the way and made so much noise that I woke Farquhar up, he began to object strenuously to what he called my "foolish anxiety about two turtles who are perfectly capable of looking after themselves".

It soon became apparent that the turtles' nocturnal restlessness was caused by the fact that they were rapidly outgrowing their washbasin. We found what seemed ideal quarters for them in a big old-fashioned bath tub which I had removed from the bathroom. It had high sides and a coffin-like taper at one end.

My Scotch friend, Jean, who was visiting at the time, and I got the tub dragged to a position just below the side veranda, cemented the inside of it and made it into what seemed to us little short of a turtle paradise. One reason for putting it where we did was that there it was close to the sea. An old-fashioned bath tub takes considerably more filling than a washbasin and that duty soon devolved on our yardboy. Feeding growing turtles becomes an onerous job after a time, too. When the girls failed to bring in sufficient shell fish, we discovered that the turtles would gladly share our food. Scones they would eat and bananas delighted them—nor did they have any objection at all to eating up as much of our monthly meat order as they could get.

When the turtles were about five years old, I made a trip to America. While I was gone, somebody stole one of them. It was a theft to be thankful for! Our solitary creature ate and swam and grew until one day I found him stuck at the narrow end of his tub, unable to turn around. I rescued him by the simple method of picking him up and putting him back into the wide end of the tub, but in a very few minutes, he was stuck again.

The bath tub was discarded and Tupou's father, Felemi, came down and dug a great circular hole into which he put a drainpipe that ran under the fence and out onto the beach. Then he cemented the pool and soon our turtle entered his spacious new home which is big enough to take care of all his future growth

Visitors with a passion for naming things are always disappointed to discover that the turtle has no name. "Flip", "Flap", "Snappy" and "Osbert" are only a few of the uninspired names they have tried to foist off on him, but he remains nameless. I say "he" merely because it is the common pronoun. It implies no knowledge of his sex. A visiting veterinarian told me that you could tell a turtles' sex by his tail. The males, he said, had longer ones, but as we have no basis for comparison, our turtle must remain, for us, sexless as well as nameless.

I advise no one to have a pet turtle. When I take guests to see ours, he swims over to the side of the pool where I am standing and tries to climb its cement sides.

" Oh, he knows you!" the visitors exclaim in delight.

Nonsense! He only knows that footsteps often precede food. His love is pure cupboard love. If I put my fingers too near his mouth which is equipped not with teeth, but with a razor sharp plate, he would quite as soon bite them off as not. On the other hand, once the trying daily task of changing his water is performed, he's an easy pet to keep. He drinks what he swims in and so long as he eats now and then, he is really not particular when he does it and has no objections at all to missing a day or two.

Nothing would induce me to have another turtle, but I should be genuinely sorry to have anything happen to the one I have. Why? I suppose because we have all grown used to him and to grow used to any living thing is to develop a sort of affection for it. When I wake in the dark lonely hours of the night, I hear his long melancholy sigh. Poor creature, I think, the world is not so bad a pool to swim in as you imagine . . . and I turn over and go to sleep until the dawn comes.

CHAPTER FOURTEEN

THE JUDGE'S STORY

ONE OF our favourite *papalangis* was the late David Hunter, a pleasant Australian, who was for many years Judge of the Supreme Court of Tonga. Whenever he was in Vava'u on circuit, he spent his weekends and spare time in 'Utulei with us. Outside of the immediate family, he was the first white person that Tami accepted. We used to say that that was because he was so dark complexioned that he could have passed for another of her beloved Tongans, but I think it must have been due rather to the basic gentleness of his nature.

On the Bench, he had an endless amount of patience which won for him the name of being a most careful and considerate judge. With that same patience and unfailing politeness, he listened to Tami's rambling childish stories and won her heart. Listening to stories was no hardship for David. He liked all sorts, but when it came to reading, he enjoyed most those dealing with his chosen profession. Because of that prediliction of his, we started to keep all the detective stories we got in the guest room and there they are still—a sort of memorial to the happy days he spent with us.

I remember one warm Sunday when Tami fell asleep over lunch and had to be carried to bed to finish her nap. Farquhar and David and I, feeling almost as sleepy, went out to the side veranda which is the coolest place in the house. Settling down in easy chairs with a book each, we read a little and talked a little until an unusually long silence was shattered by David's book crashing to the floor. He sat up with a start, retrieved the book and said, " I'm sorry. I guess I was nodding."

" It's not everyone," Farquhar said, " who can catch Justice nodding."

David laughed. " I'll tell you a story about the time I was

caught napping on the Bench," he said. " It was on just such a hot drowsy afternoon as this that I was hearing a case over in Neiafu. It was an assault case and it seemed to me the most cut-and-dried one imaginable. A man called Tailu was riding his bicycle along the road to Makave, his home village."

David paused for long enough to light a fresh cigarette and then went on, " He'd passed that big frangipani tree—you know the one with all the pink flowers, and was just going by the cemetery when a fellow called Mosese who had long had a grudge against him, rose out of a clump of red hibiscus bushes. Evidently he'd been lying in wait for him. He ran out and kicked the bicycle so that Tailu fell to the ground. Before he could get up, Mosese set to and gave him a regular beating. When he'd finished, he ran off, leaving the wounded Tailu beside the road where, shortly afterwards, he was found by a villager and taken to the hospital. Mosese had really knocked him about badly. He had a broken leg and severe body lacerations and bruises. Naturally the doctors reported the matter and before long the police arrived at Tailu's bedside and took a statement from him. That same night they picked Mosese up.

" He was drunk when they got him. Once he had cooled off, he'd begun to fear the consequences of his actions and was bolstering up his courage at a kava party. It wasn't quite the usual village kava party. Added to the Tongan kava was some kava *papalangi*—the rot-gut stuff that the stores sell out of a barrel. Mosese had had just enough of it to give him a false sense of courage.

" When the police arrived, he swaggered up to them and asked them what they wanted. Quite as he expected, they said they wanted him. Proudly he drew himself up to his full height, threw back his head and said, 'I know. You're after me for beating up that worthless Tailu'.

" The police agreed that that was why they were there. They tossed him into the Landrover and as they rode along to jail, he regaled them all with a full account of the clever way in which he had surprised and beaten Tailu. Completely unrepentant, he boasted of his strength and 'Look at me', he said, 'Not a scratch anywhere'."

David turned towards us. " Those were the facts," he said. " It really didn't seem like a case at all. Mosese was guilty and he had admitted it. Nothing remained but the formalities of the trial and the sentence and, as I said before, it was a drowsy afternoon like this one."

Then David added slowly, as if to emphasise the point, "There was just one thing that should have warned me. Mosese's lawyer was Fisihoi."

Farquhar's eyes had just fallen shut, but he opened them at once. "So the case was not so simple after all," he said and from then on his eyes stayed open. So did mine. Fisihoi was perhaps the most brilliant and most colourful lawyer that Tonga has ever produced. A big man, even in this country of big men, he towered far above ordinary people. His thick white hair and his dignified grave manner made him seem the very embodiment of justice. Educated in Australia, he had learned his law thoroughly. He had, moreover, a nimble mind that could fit the most disconnected bits of evidence together like jigsaw puzzle pieces. His greatest joy lay in manipulating both the law and people's minds to prove that his client—whoever he was and whatever he had done, was completely innocent.

"Well," said David, taking up his story again. "Everyone in court that day was fanning himself and mopping his brow. There I sat stifling in my robes and wig trying to look dignified and trying even harder to stay awake until it was time to sentence Mosese. Fisihoi is brilliant, but sometimes he can be terribly boring."

"The two often go together," Farquhar remarked.

David agreed. "They did in this case. First he had Tailu up and exhibited his wounds, explaining at great length how serious and how painful each one was. Frankly, it seemed a strange thing for the defence lawyer to be doing—but after all, the wounds were so obvious that they couldn't very easily have been overlooked. I thought Fisihoi was feeling the heat as much as I was and had decided to plead his client guilty at once and get it over with—but no such luck!

"He went on and on in that maddening way of his, probing into every slightest detail, asking Tailu all sorts of questions which, to my mind, were totally irrelevant, but Tailu's lawyer didn't object and I'm afraid I wasn't able to. My eyes were open and I nodded my head every now and then as if I were considering a point, but the truth of the matter is, I had dozed off.

" I came to with a start when I heard Tailu's lawyer—a meek little man, crying out like a trapped rabbit, " I object. I object, Your Honour."

" As you know, I always sit in court with an interpreter. My Tongan is improving, but it's not yet good enough to be trusted when it's a question of a man's life—or even of his goods."

David took a few puffs on his cigarette and watched the smoke curl lazily away before he went on. " Among his other uses an interpreter can disguise the fact that I've had a snooze. He certainly did then. I leaned over and said, 'Please let me have that in English'.

" From his notes, the interpreter read, 'Fisihoi: Your Honour, I submit that the prosecution has no case because Tailu received no wounds from my client'."

" 'Masi: 'I object. I object, Your Honour'."

David laughed apologetically. " I must confess I love to hear old Fisihoi argue when he's in form. I knew, of course, that Mosese hadn't been sober when he confessed and I supposed Fisihoi had proved that he was incapable of confessing. Probably he'd come up with an unknown assailant. He's very clever at that sort of thing. At any rate, I had to cover up the fact that I'd been asleep; so I said, 'We'd better have the whole defence over in English.'

" So Fisihoi had Tailu up again. I yawned through what seemed like a lot of tiresome repetition, but I stayed awake. I couldn't help myself. The interpreter stood at my side turning all the proceedings into his old staccato English. After a time, Fisihoi asked, 'And where were you when this alleged attack occurred?'

" Tailu explained that he had turned off the main road, passed the frangipani tree and was just going by the cemetery when Mosese sprang out of the bushes at him."

" 'And what kind of bushes were they?' Fisihoi demanded.

" 'Hibiscus bushes.'

" 'And what colour were they?'

" 'Common red ones.'

" 'Fisihoi smiled triumphantly as if Tailu had made a great admission and asked, ' And exactly where were those bushes? Were they in the cemetery or were they on the opposite side of the road?'

" 'They were in the cemetery itself.'

" 'Hmm,' said Fisihoi as he took out the great white silk handkerchief that he always kept folded in his breast pocket and thoughtfully wiped his brow with it. When he spoke again, it seemed to me that he was off on what I always think of as one of his famous *non sequiturs*. ' Do you play cards?' he asked.

" Tailu admitted that he did."

" 'And do you sometimes tell fortunes with cards?'

" 'Sometimes I do,' Tailu said and it was obvious that he was proud that his skill was known.

" 'Is it true,' Fisihoi continued, ' that on the week before the attack you went to a kava party and told fortunes for everyone there?'

" ' That is true,' Tailu said and I wondered wearily where all this was leading to.

" I did not have long to wonder. Fisihoi dismissed Tailu, turned to me and said, ' With your permission, Your Honour, I shall now give my summing up directly in English so you will not have to be unduly delayed on this hot day.'

" I thanked him and gave my consent."

" He spoke briefly to the jury in Tongan, explaining to them that they had already heard his summing up. He begged them to be patient while he repeated it in English for me and implored them to remember what he was sure they could not forget—that Mosese was completely innocent. Then he turned, bowed slightly in my direction and said, ' Your Honour.' "

David looked up at us. " I've known Fisihoi for a long time," he said. " I know what a clever old bag of tricks he is, but there's something about the way he addresses the Bench that gets me every time. ' Your Honour,' he says it in such a voice that makes me feel just for the minute of hearing it that it would be impossible ever to disagree with him. He's an artist who holds one in what Coleridge called a willing suspension of disbelief.

" That day he started out mildly enough. ' We are Christians . . . you and I,' he began. ' We know that man is small and God is great. We live our little lives from day to day, but only God knows the great overall plan He has for each one of us.' "

David explained, " Like most Tongan men, Fisihoi is a lay preacher. I was afraid I was in for a full length sermon. I'm not much for sermons at any time and . . . well, my attention wandered. When I came to again, Fisihoi was talking of his people's old beliefs in spirits, but instead of speaking of them in the past, he spoke as if they were very much in the present."

"So they are for most Tongans," Farquhar put in.

"That's true," David said, "but Fisihoi knows better. He doesn't believe in spirits any more than you and I do, but there he was talking about them as if they were real as the pots in the kitchen.

"'Your Honour,' he said, 'everyone knows that the spirits live on in the cemetery. The spirits know things that are hidden to living man. They know the past.' Fisihoi stopped for a full minute before he continued on in measured tones . . . 'And they know the future. Now, how do you think they feel when some ordinary little man . . .' and he turned and stared at Tailu who squirmed and looked away. 'How do you think they feel when such a person tries to take over their work and foretells the future? How would you feel if someone tried to deprive us of work God fitted us to do? Perhaps if such a terrible thing were to happen to us, we would be powerless to fight against it . . . but, Oh! Your Honour, the spirits are strong, very strong. They can do things man cannot do. And they are full of vengeance. It was a very simple thing for those spirits whom Tailu had wronged by trying to foretell the future to assume the shape of Mosese.

"'I ask you, could any mere man have inflicted on an able-bodied Tongan the grievous wounds Tailu suffered without himself showing the least scratch? And Mosese had no scratch. Why? Because he never attacked Tailu. Obviously, it was the spirits.'

"Fisihoi stepped back, took out his white handkerchief once more, flourished it over his forehead and went on in the patient tone of voice one uses to explain things to a child. 'You may tell me, Your Honour, that Mosese has confessed, but was it Mosese? You know very well that no Tongan ever confesses of his own free will. Certainly no Tongan is so foolish as to boast to the police of having committed a crime.'

"Fisihoi leaned forward, gave me a conspiratorial smile and asked, 'Do you want to know what really happened, Your Honour?'

"The question was a purely rhetorical one. He hurried on at once. 'I'll tell you. My client, Mosese, is a sober, honest, hard-working man. If he has a fault at all, it is that he works too hard.' He pointed dramatically to Mosese who, when I looked at him, lowered his head with befitting modesty.

"'He works too hard,' Fisihoi repeated. 'That's exactly what had happened on the day we are discussing. He'd been to the bush. All day he'd worked planting yams. The other men had gone home at mid-day for some food and a rest, but not Mosese. He kept right on until every yam was in the ground. Only then did he think about going home. But, Your Honour, fine man though he is, Mosese is only human. He was tired, exhausted. By the time he'd reached the cemetery, he felt he couldn't go on another step. If he hadn't been so tired, he'd never have stopped at such a place, but when he saw those old red hibiscus bushes, he forgot all about the cemetery and just crept in behind them to sleep awhile. And what happened then? Why, the simplest thing in the world. The angry spirits borrowed his body. They waited for Tailu and they beat him up, they went to that kava party and got disgracefully drunk, they boasted to the police, they spent the night in jail, they were charged with the crime, they were not released the next morning until time for the trial. It wasn't until the morning when they got back to the cemetery and gave Mosese's body back to him, that he woke up and went on home, the same innocent man he's always been.'"

I interrupted, "What a lot of nonsense!"

David agreed with me. "But you should have seen Tailu," he said. "The big lawyer turned, shook his fist at him and cried, 'That beating up was only the warning. The spirits have not given up. If this misguided man continues to pry into the future, let him beware. The spirits have wounded him. They can do more. They can kill.' Fisihoi was speaking in English, but obviously Tailu had heard the same thing in Tongan. He knew all too well what was being said. I saw him begin to shake. He turned so white I was afraid he was going to faint. Then Fisihoi was saying, 'That is my case, Your Honour.'"

David stopped, rubbed the side of his cheek in a meditative way and said in a puzzled tone, "Fisihoi is pure magic. While he's talking, you can't help believing whatever mad thing he says. Actually, I should have kept on believing him, but as soon as he had stopped talking, I said just as you do, 'What a lot of nonsense!' I sent the jury out and when I gave them my instructions, I never even mentioned Fisihoi's summing up. It seemed too foolish for anyone to consider seriously."

"And what happened?" Farquhar and I asked together.

"Just what any Tongan could have told you would happen," David said. "Mosese was acquitted and back he went to the village boasting that the spirits were on his side."

"And what of Tailu?" we asked.

David shook his head. "Poor fellow," he said. "He's given up telling fortunes. He shakes whenever he sees Mosese and, as for the spirits, he takes no chances with them. He bicycles home the long way around so he won't have to pass the cemetery again."

CHAPTER FIFTEEN

ON PRECONCEIVED NOTIONS

About the islands—as about other things, most of my preconceived notions, even those that were most strongly supported by reading or by other people's experiences, have turned out to be wrong. One I treasure because it turned out to be exactly right.

On a day long ago before ever I saw the tropics, I was staying at Lake Tahoe, high in the Sierras of my native California. With some friends, I was making a trip on the all-day excursion steamer that used to circle the lake. When we set out, the day was cloudless, the sun shining with midsummer intensity, but just before we got to Emerald Bay a quick scud of clouds filled the sky. As we began to go around the island in the bay, the bright green water darkened and the rain began to fall. Before it had been raining long, the sun broke through the clouds, but the rain continued. Suddenly, as if the sun had fallen into the depths of the lake and was shining up through them, the water turned into a brilliant, translucent green sheet on which danced the silver bells of raindrops.

Filled with the beauty of the day, I turned to the friend at my side. " I think," I said, " that the tropics must be like this."

And I was right. Now when there is such a day—and there are many during our rainy season, I put on my bathing suit and run down to the beach and into the sea. Falling on the water, the raindrops sound like a thousand fairy pea-pods being popped all at once. The sea itself, as if lit by submarine flood lights glows with a rare golden iridescence. If I stop swimming for a minute and float quietly in the water, I can feel the tiny splash of fresh water as the silver bells, wearying of floating, pop and disappear into the sea.

I look directly across the harbour. Talau mountain, a dark green mass, rises from the sea, its strange, truncated top half hidden by low clouds. Beyond it, stretching up its sides are the red-roofed houses of Neiafu. If I turn and swim toward the sunset, I see the long green channel of the harbour with islands rising on either side and far far down, at the foot of the harbour, protecting it from the wild open sea, is rocky Kitu against whose breadloaf sides there is always a high rush of white surf.

I turn and swim again, with my eyes shut this time and I see Tahoe the Lake of the Sky. I am back on the steamer with all my gay young friends. We are rounding Emerald Bay and I feel a rush of pleasure. It is like the tropics, like my own 'Utulei. For once, my preconceived notion was correct.

I think it must be one of the gifts of the years that beauty is not single, but like some magic mirrored room reflects endlessly back until the glory of Tahoe and the joy I knew on that distant day are forever a part of and an intensification of the green-gold days I know here.

CHAPTER SIXTEEN

THE HAUNTED HOUSE

Not many days after David had told his story of the spirits that upset his court, Farquhar came home from the hospital and I ran down the beach to meet him.

"Any news of the town?" I asked as he got out of the boat and threw the anchor far up the sandy beach.

"No," he said and added after a minute, "except . . ."

"Except what?" and I looked up to see that his eyes were twinkling and his face was creasing into a laugh.

"Except that I've got the end of our haunted house serial for you."

"Tell me," I insisted, but he had already crossed the beach and gone into the garden. "I'll have a cup of tea first," he said.

For months the haunted house had been the main topic of conversation in all of Vava'u. Because its story came to us a little at a time, we had long since come to refer to it among ourselves as "our serial" and eagerly we awaited each new instalment.

The house itself was over in Neiafu—a big old time Tongan *fale* of the sort one seldom sees nowadays with close-woven reed walls and a thick thatched roof that hung so low over the single door that the whole inside was plunged into eternal gloom. There was little enough to see in there, anyway, and nothing to remark on. It was like a thousand other old *fales* with the family's bed rolls on the floor, a basket or two of food or small possessions hanging from the house-poles and, up in the rafters, the rolls of *tapa* and mats that constituted the wealth of the household. But that unlikely place had, for months past, been haunted. The ghosts who had taken up residence there were no ordinary polite spirits, nor were they content with the usual groanings and rattlings of chains. Aggressive modern ghosts they were who worked by day as well as by night, manifesting themselves by the disgusting habit of spitting on everyone who dared to enter their house.

If the spirits of the haunted house were unusual members of the ghostly clan, so likewise was Tina, the woman of the house, an a-typical Tongan. Here where most men and women accept their good health as naturally as they except the sunshine, Tina spent a large part of her time trying to convince herself and the medical department that she suffered from a series of dreadful ailments. Time and time again Farquhar had left important work at the hospital to answer her frantic calls and never had he found her suffering from anything more serious than a case of sniffles or a cut finger. Just a few weeks before her house started being haunted, she had again sent word to the hospital. She was dying. She must see Farquhar at once. His morning schedule of operations was almost ready to begin, but he called Kupu, the driver, who brought the old Landrover around and hurtled him down the hill to Tina's house. When he went in to her, it was so obvious that— far from being moribund, she was the possessor of the most robust and enviable good health that his Scotch patience came to an end. " Get up at once," he said angrily. " Go about your business and stop disturbing mine. Nothing's wrong with you. Nothing at all." And he strode out of her house.

Under the circumstances, it was scarcely surprising that when Tina next fell a prey to a newly imagined disease—one which, furthermore, was badly aggravated by the arrival in her house of the spirits, she specifically requested that Farquhar stay away. She preferred, she said, to see Lutui, the MO. He, being Tongan, would be more sympathetic.

So down Lutui went and listened patiently while she recited a long list of symptoms and an even longer list of the trials attendant on living in a house peopled by spitting spirits.

As a matter of strict medical interest, it must be reported that Lutui found no more wrong with her than Farquhar had done. Furthermore, as a medical man, he had no belief in spirits, but it must be confessed that, as a Tongan he had—well, an interest in them.

He muttered soothing words to Tina, gave her a placebo and was preparing to come away when—plop, on the middle of his forehead, he received something which made him uncomfortably aware that, whether he believed in them or not, the spirits had spat on him. Indignantly, he wiped his forehead and, hurrying back to the hospital, reported to Farquhar what had happened.

"You know," Farquhar had said when he told me about it, "Lutui doesn't really believe in ghosts. He knows better, but sometimes he forgets what he knows."

"What's he going to do about it?" I asked.

"I've advised him," Farquhar said in his most serious professional voice, "to take a slide the next time he goes to that house and collect a specimen of the sputum."

"And what good is that going to do?"

Farquhar smiled knowingly. "Wait and see."

A few days later, I heard that Lutui had collected his specimen and taken it back to the laboratory at the hospital where Maile, the technician, had analysed it. Far from exhibiting any other worldly components, it contained all the characteristics and all the bacteria of normal human sputum.

Science triumphed over the shadows as Lutui, the report in his hand, went to Farquhar and confessed, "Doctor, as a Tongan I can understand ghosts. I can even understand rare ghosts who spit but as a MO I can't understand ghostly sputum being full of normal human bacteria."

When Farquhar asked him what he intended to do about it, Lutui laughed. "I shall pursue the matter scientifically," he said, "and on the basis of Maile's findings and Newton's law of gravity, investigate the phenomenon thoroughly."

And that is as far as the story had gone on the day that Farquhar came home and told me he had the end of our serial and would tell me after he had had a cup of tea. I had learned by then to quell my American impatience before his ever present Scotch need for a cup of tea; so I followed him meekly into the house and waited while he took off his hat, waited while he washed his hands, waited while he went to the veranda and settled into an easy chair, waited while—the cup of tea having been brought to him—he sugared and creamed it and stirred, waited still as he sipped experimentally and then, having found it to his liking, drank it off in great gulps of satisfaction. Only when he had set the cup firmly down on its saucer, did I ask again, "What happened? How does the story end?"

"This morning," he began then, "Tina sent one of her sons to the hospital with a note to say she was sick again and wanted to see Lutui. He went, but this time, he didn't go alone. He rounded up the hospital gardener and the caretaker and the boy that tends the pump. On the way downtown, he stopped at his own house and got the old war club that belonged to his great great grandfather and talked a few of his cousins who happened to be there into going along with him."

"When they arrived at Tina's, he got out of the Rover and went in to see his patient just as he'd always done, but once he was inside, the others, as had been arranged, followed quietly and surrounded the house.

"Inside, Tina had new symptoms and old complaints with which to regale Lutui. She was especially vehement about her ghosts who, she said, were driving away all her friends. Lutui's bedside manner was never better. He listened with sympathetic bent head, he consoled her, he expressed amazement at the number and variety of trials she was called on to bear, he prescribed potions and pills and rubbing ointment. And when he got up to leave, his fee was once again a large gob of spit right in the middle of his forehead.

"No sooner had it fallen on him than he cried out in a loud voice. ' Whoever did that, come here at once '.

"Ghosts aren't accustomed to answering humans, so naturally there was no response, but Lutui called out again, summoning his helpers to draw closer to the house and shouting to them to give him his great-grandfather's club.

"When he had it in his hand, he reached up and began methodically beating about in the dark rafters above him. A rain of dust showered down. He hit one big roll of *tapa* and the cord that was holding it burst and *tapa* came spilling out all over the floor.

"Tina forgetting her sickness, sprang out of bed, grasped Lutui's arm and cried, ' What are you doing to my house? Are you mad? You're ruining the place'.

"He pushed her away as easily as if she had been one of her own ghosts. ' Keep out of my way,' he shouted at her. ' I'm making a scientific experiment,' and he went on beating at the gloomy darkness above him. More dust fell and more and with it came a tinkling rain of lopa seeds and little necklace cowries that someone had long ago shoved into an old basket that hung in the shadows. And still Lutui beat at the rafters with his mighty club until the whole house shook. At last there was a dull thud as he pounded a great roll of mats and a second as he hit it again, followed by a seismic blast as it hit the floor and unrolled, revealing in its centre two tousled and giggling boys."

Farquhar paused for a moment before he said, " They didn't giggle for long. Lutui gave a great shout to his friends to come in and see the ghosts and reaching out, caught one of the boys and gave him a good thrashing. The other was quicker and ran away, but one of Lutui's cousins grabbed him as he tried to get out the door and flung him back to Lutui who gave him a thrashing, too. As for Tina, she got only a piece of Lutui's mind, but somehow, I think it will be a long time before the medical department hears from her again."

" And what's the moral of that tale?"

" Why," Farquhar smiled, " I suppose that ghosts are the same the world over."

" Or that small boys are."

" Or," he concluded with a sigh, " that neurotic women who plague doctors flourish everywhere."

CHAPTER SEVENTEEN

MISCONCEPTIONS, TONGAN AND *PAPALANGI*

SOMETIMES, LISTENING to the nightly radio reports of ever-growing international disputes, I wonder how people can fail to comprehend one another as often as they do. Then I think of all the innocent misunderstandings that go on around here between Tongans and *papalangis*—two groups of people who, on the whole, live happily and peacefully together, and I begin to understand how the world at large gets into so many muddles.

Take, for instance, the question of work. Most white men, when they think of islanders, imagine a pleasant brown-skinned fellow who dreams his life away sleeping beneath a swaying coconut tree. Nothing could be further from the truth. Quite aside from the fact that no sensible Tongan would nap beneath a coconut where he would be in constant danger of having his brains dashed out by falling nuts, most men here find little time for naps at all. In mid-life an ordinary man is likely to find himself with a household that, in addition to his wife, includes eight or nine children, at least one set of elderly parents, a stray aunt or uncle, a brace of cousins and a few more distant relatives. Providing food, shelter, and clothes for all of them and paying school fees for the young ones is no job for a sluggard. A man must spend long days in the bush planting food if he is to keep the pot that boils in his open air kitchen filled and other long days cutting copra if he is to get the money necessary for the things he buys from the store. It is true that the Tongan earth is fertile, but it is an impartial fertility which pours forth weeds as abundantly as food crops. To fight them, local farmers have only simple hand tools—a hoe, a bush knife, a yam planter. It is a battle which can well be waged from dawn to dusk.

Lack of understanding is not, however, purely a *papalangi*

failing. Tongans, on their side, firmly believe that white men rarely work, and that the possession of an unending supply of money is a natural state with them.

One of the most interesting books I have ever read about Tonga was written by the New Zealand husband-wife anthropological team, Pearl and Ernest Beaglehole. Titled, *Pangai: Village in Tonga*, it is a study of the daily lives of average people in a typical village—a thorough and perceptive study which represents a great deal of good hard work. Pangai, as it happens, is on the same island as 'Utulei and there is much coming and going between the two villages so the book has a more than ordinary interest for me. When I discovered that Silia, the college girl who lived with me during the year I taught at Siuilikutapu College, came from Pangai and that it was in her home that the Beagleholes had stayed, I was interested in discovering how they worked.

"What did they do all day?" I asked Silia.

She smiled and shrugged her shoulders. "Nothing," she said.

When I pressed her, she could only add that they walked around and talked to people and swam and amused themselves. Her reply, of course, in addition to revealing a complete lack of comprehension on her part, is a great tribute to the Beagleholes who were able to elicit the information which enabled them to reproduce a whole society without giving its members the slightest hint of what was going on.

A Tongan friend of mine once explained our differences by remarking casually, "We Tongans have land, *papalangis* have money." Nothing can dislodge that idea from the Tongan mind, nor can they be convinced that our money is sometimes very hard come by. When I told the same friend that the money which I received from the sale of my book *Tonga: A Tale of the Friendly Islands* was to be set aside for the girls' education, she exclaimed innocently, "How fortunate you are to be able to get money without doing any work."

CHAPTER EIGHTEEN

THE HURRICANE

ONE WEDNESDAY night Farquhar went to bed early; but when, after an hour or so, I shut my book and followed him, I found him still awake.

"This is a terribly noisy house," he murmured as I went into the bedroom. "It sounds nervous tonight."

His words were apt. The house did sound nervous. It cracked and creaked in every joist and beam and overhead the strange "steps" that make my Tongan friends say the place is haunted kept walking back and forth. Outside the window, a bit of loose guttering flapped metallically in the wind while I turned and twisted on the bed trying vainly to find a comfortable sleeping position. At last I gave up and lay on my back, staring with eyes wide open, but unseeing into the blackness that filled the room. It seemed as if I had been lying there for dark eons when I heard Farquhar whisper, "Are you still awake?"

"Yes."

"I'm tired of lying here and not sleeping. Let's get up and make some tea."

We got up and lit the lamp. While Farquhar was pumping the Primus stove, I went about closing the shutters to keep out the dark windy night. Usually in our midnight sessions, we discussed the books that we had been reading before we went to bed or the events of the day, but that night we were both too restless to settle into any real conversation. Our sporadic talk was punctuated by the sound of branches flailing against the iron roof, by banging doors, by Tupou moaning in her sleep . . . until at last we sat, unspeaking and tense, listening to the noises of the night. Finally Farquhar said, "The wind is rising." As if to emphasise his words, an especially strong gust found its way through the closed shutters and set the flames of the lamp trembling into smoke. Seeing it, he shrugged his shoulders, " If the lamp's going to misbehave, we might as well go back to bed and try to get some sleep. I think it will be light before we know it."

Tired though we were when we returned to bed, our sleep was, at best, fitful, full of strange dreams and sudden wakings. Once I heard waves splashing angrily against the sea wall. Would the line of frangipani trees at the edge of the garden be safe, I wondered. They were only a few feet from the sea—and what of my hibiscus, the delicate orange one whose tapered petals made the flowers seem bright stars dotting the green foliage. Because it was one of my own hybrids, I felt for it the protective pride of a creator. Would the sea spray hurt it? Half-asleep, half-awake, I tossed and turned the hours away, but the light Farquhar had predicted did not come. In its place a heavy greyness oozed slowly over the earth and surged into the bedroom. Farquhar had fallen into the deep sleep of exhaustion, but weary of bed, I crept silently out, got dressed quickly and ran against the wind into the garden.

Like heavy-headed dolls, the whole line of frangipani trees had toppled over and lay on their sides with the wind tearing at their already wilted leaves and flowers. Over the sea wall, the waves came flooding in as they had never done before. I looked for my prize orange hibiscus and discovered it fallen, its roots exposed by the dirty swirling sea water. As best I could I propped it up and made a protective wall of rocks and mud around it. A single perfect star had struggled into bloom. Leaving it to make a spot of brightness in that dull morning, I started back to the house. As I passed the work house, I saw that the door was open and someone was inside; so I went to investigate. There I found Tupou's father, Felemi.

" I'm looking for roofing nails," he explained. " My roof is working loose in the wind."

Pulling down boxes and tins, I helped him look, making as I did so, small talk about the weather. Suddenly he turned to me, " Didn't you listen to the radio last night?" he asked.

I shook my head. " No. We were reading or talking and news time slipped by before we realised it. Why?"

" Hurricane," he said. " The warning for Vava'u was on the radio last night. It's headed right for us."

He had found his nails, but he stopped a minute to warn me. "You'd better get ready," and with that, he ran out of the building and up the hill to his house.

For a minute I stood watching him. How did one get ready for a hurricane? I had no idea. Some people put up storm shutters, but we had none. When knowing visitors had asked us about storms, we had always assured them that our house on the beach with the village hill rising behind it and the cemetery hill curving around to form a little bay on the side, was in a pocket of safety. In any event, a hurricane had been, like the giants that used to live down the harbour and devour passing boatmen something that belonged to Tonga's past. Now I was not so sure. Back in the kitchen I found Langa'ola, the housegirl, weeping silently as she got out the breakfast things.

"What is it?" I asked, expecting a report of some domestic woe, but she only shook her head and said between sobs, "Afa . . . afa." So I learned the Tongan word for hurricane. It was one I was never to forget.

Farquhar was in the living-room standing before the picture window with one arm around Tami and the other around Tupou. They turned as I came in and he said, "Look at that sea. It's much too wild for me to try to get across to the hospital today. I could never steer the boat through that."

I told him then Felemi's news. His face grew grave and troubled and Tami and Tupou moved closer to him. Sensing their fright, he began to move forward, saying in his matter of fact voice, "I think I heard the breakfast bell."

After a hasty meal, Farquhar went off to the beach to help the village men who had gathered to pull up the boats. I followed him as far as the school house at the foot of the garden. I knew we could not possibly have school down there on such a windy day, so I loaded my arms with books that I carried back to the house.

"We'd better come and help you and bring everything up," Tami said as I put the books down on the dining-room table.

"Come on then," I said and she and Tupou, laughing because the wind blew so hard against them that they staggered drunkenly as they ran across the lawn, carried notebooks and crayons and the big blue globe while I brought the remainder of the books.

When all our school materials had been transferred to the

dining-room, we sat down at the big table to begin the day's first lesson—arithmetic. We made little progress. Before we had solved one problem, we were yelling at the tops of our voices trying to make ourselves heard over the howl of the wind and the crash of branches falling on the roof above our heads. Nevertheless, we kept doggedly on with the hopeless class until a sudden thud burst like a cannon ball on the roof above our heads. Startled, I looked up and stared straight into Tupou's brown eyes. They were stretched wide with fear. Another cannon ball blasted overhead. Tami's green eyes were misted with terror. Going to the window, I saw the big unripe fruit of the avocado tree being ripped by the wind from its branches and flung down on the roof. "It's only the avocado," I said to the girls. "There's nothing to be afraid of," and sitting down at the table again, I tried to go on with the lesson. It was a futile attempt. The avocado bombardment continued until it seemed the roof must collapse over our heads. Nor did it add to our composure to have Langa'ola, when she had finished the breakfast dishes, come and stand silently in the doorway while big tears rolled down her plump cheeks.

Recognising that school had become an impossibility, I shouted over the noise to the girls, "All right. Shut your books. We won't have school today. We'll all go to Tami's room." Such an announcement would usually have resulted in shouts of joy, but the girls heard it apathetically and did not move until I stood up and herded them—and Langa'ola with them—out of the dining-room and down the hall.

Wedged in between the guest room and hall, Tami's room was the most sheltered in the house and by far the quietest. I told the girls to sit down on the mat in the centre of the room. When they were settled, I brought out a big jigsaw puzzle that they had been begging me to let them do. "There it is," I said, spreading the pieces over the mat. "See how quickly you can put it together."

The three of them sat staring dully down at the puzzle, making not the slightest move. "Go on," I said, "start." Tami picked up a piece, stared blankly at it for a minute and listlessly let it fall out of her hand. Langa'ola tried in a half-hearted way to force together two pieces that obviously didn't fit. Tupou did not even pretend to be interested. "What's the matter with you?" I cried, starting to grow angry at their lack of response to my efforts to amuse them. "I thought you wanted to do this puzzle."

Without bothering to lift her head, Tami said, "You can't do jigsaw puzzles in the dark."

I looked down and saw that she was right. It was quite impossible to tell one piece from another; for, on that strange day, it was growing increasingly darker as the morning progressed. I swept the pieces back into their box, but I was still determined to try to keep the girls' minds off the storm.

"Let's listen to a record," I said brightly and, finding the gayest tune in the house, put it on Tami's little player and set it going. Against the muted storm it tinkled in a nervous funereal counterpoint. "Turn it off. Turn it off," Tami demanded.

Then I was forced to realise that there are times in life when neither arithmetic, nor jigsaw puzzles, nor music, nor any other thing will help. Such times must simply be endured. There in Tami's room, they were as safe as they could be anywhere. I went out and left them to endure.

Farquhar had come up from the beach and gone into the library where he was listening to the weather news on the radio. He snapped it off as I came in and said, "The report has just come through that the eye of the storm is due to pass over us at noon. Until then, we can expect the wind to get worse."

It got worse almost at once. The rain which, up to that time had held off, began to fall. Before it reached the ground, it was caught up by the wind, mixed with sharp bits of sand and transformed into hard dirty spume which pricked against the house like a thousand miniature machine guns.

Suddenly Farquhar touched me on the arm to attract by attention and shouted, "What's that?"

Beneath all the wild noise of the storm was a familiar homely sound ... a steady persistent knocking from the direction of the kitchen. "It sounds like someone knocking on the back door. I'll go and see."

Not wanting to let the wind in, I opened the door only a tiny crack. Before it stood Mata'aisi, the village school teacher. Polite as always, he asked, "May these people come in?" and standing aside pointed to where my old housegirl, Nia, grown up now, stood with her mother and father and sisters and brothers. "Their home has collapsed," he explained.

"Come in—all of you, quickly," I called and held the door until the last of them was in. The little ones were soaking wet and shivering with cold and fright. " Sit by the stove and get warm," I said and went off to find some dry clothes for them. While they were putting them on, we heard how, when a particularly strong blast of wind had knocked their own house into a shambles of broken wood, they had run to the church for shelter. No sooner had they got inside than the church walls began to sway. When, a second later, the roof was whipped off, they ran out just before the whole thing crashed. Mata'aisi had found them there shocked and huddled beside the wreckage and led them down to us. I took them into Tami's room where the girls and Langa'ola were sitting just where I had left them, holding pillows to their heads to shut out the noise of the storm.

When they were settled, I went back to the kitchen. Mata'aisi followed me. He picked up an old basket that was standing under the meat safe. " I'll take this," he said, " and go and gather up the fallen breadfruit and avocados for you."

" They're much too green," I said, but he smiled. " They will be needed even so," and opening the door, slipped out. Before it had closed again, Felemi appeared. " The nails didn't hold the roof," he said forlornly. " It's gone and all the house with it. Can I bring my family here?"

" Certainly," I said, " bring them down," but they were down already, right behind him and as soon as I had spoken, they came crowding in at the door.

Those first comers—Nia and her family and Felemi and his, had knocked at the door and asked politely if they could come in, but as time went on and the storm raged ever wilder, such civilities were dispensed with. At intervals, the door was pushed open as, one after another of the village families poured into the house seeking refuge. Soon they filled Tami's room, spilled out along the hallways and filled, too, the dining-room, living-room and kitchen. They did not go into our room. On one trip that I made into it to search for some dry clothes for newcomers, I discovered it had ceased to exist. The roof had gone and one of the walls had fallen, but the row of sturdy cupboards that had been made for us by Jack Hoel, the old Norwegian carpenter, stood like Vikings against the storm. Nor did they go into Tupou's room where a flying board had been driven through the window, filling the room with splinters of broken glass and letting in the wind and the rain.

In the parts of the house that remained habitable there were—

when they were all in, 143 villagers. When they came, they were wet and many of the children were naked. Some came empty handed. Others carried a basket containing a few clothes or a bit of food. A few came with all their treasures—their Bibles, clocks and lamps. There was even a sewing machine and a Primus or two.

All told the same tale. Their roofs had been ripped off and the walls of their homes had collapsed about them. One small boy had leapt from a window just as the walls started to fall. He had been caught up by the wind and carried over half the village before his frantic mother had been able to catch up with him and grab him from the dark sky.

At noon, as the radio had predicted, the eye of the storm passed directly over us. The wind died in a calm that—eerie and ominous as it was, made us feel a new distrust in nature. Most of the women and children stayed huddled together inside, but when I saw the men going out, I followed them.

We entered an ugly world. My beautiful green Vava'u had disappeared. Every leaf had been stripped from tree and bush and plant and the wind-driven sea spray had turned the grass a sickly yellow. I picked my way through the rubble that littered the garden and went to look for my prized orange hibiscus. The whole plant must have been carried away. I could not find the smallest part of it, nor did I think of it again for a long time because, as suddenly as it had died away, the wind rose again. Bracing myself against it, I ran back into the house. Farquhar was reassuring. "The centre has passed," he said. "The wind will be dying away soon."

Reassuring though he was, he was wrong. In the afternoon there was another brief lull. Then the wind began blowing from the opposite direction. The villagers murmured to one another and Farquhar and I exchanged glances. He shook his head. "I don't like this," and went off to the radio. Our worst fears were soon confirmed. The storm, which at first had travelled north, had now turned completely around and, going south, was once more headed directly for us.

Before the afternoon was over the roof of the library blew off and the rain came pouring in. Hurriedly, I organised relay teams of people to move the books into the hall which was comparatively dry, although no place in the house was truly so because the wind drove the rain in under the sheets of iron roofing so that, through the ceiling, there was a constant fine drizzle. The book lift proved to be a godsend to the morale of our group. Soon all the men and women were involved and Tami and Tupou and the other children had taken their heads out of their pillows and were helping, taking armfuls of books out of the shelves, passing them along from one to another until they reached the hallway where they were stacked in neat piles. Tongans cannot work without talking and they cannot talk without laughing and singing. It was good to hear their gaiety rising above the storm. Later I learned that in many places where people had had nothing to do but sit and tremble at each fresh blast of wind, many of them had lost all control of themselves and given way to hysteria. Fortunately our group was far too busy and far too merry for that.

The exercise involved in the book lift presented us with another problem. It was not long before the children began clamouring for something to eat and the grown-ups confessed to an interior emptiness. The teacher, Mata'aisi, who all day long had been busy getting each new family as it came in, settled, and in keeping everyone content, volunteered to help me get dinner. It was no simple project. Early in the morning, the chimney had crashed to the ground so there was no question of using the big stove. Whatever we cooked, it would have to be done on the single plate of the Primus.

Fortunately, just the week before when I had decided that with Tami and Tupou both consuming milk like two thirsty young calves, it was economically unsound to buy milk powder a tin at a time, I had bought a case. I also had a case of tinned fish. The supplies determined the menu—creamed fish and cocoa for the adults, milk for the babies. We prepared the food in big canning pots which we managed to balance on top of the Primus and, as we did not have plates enough for all, simply served one big plate to each family group. Mata'aisi saw that everyone got his just share and that after one group had eaten, the dishes were gathered and washed for the next eaters. It was not by any means a well balanced meal and such amenities as knives, forks, and spoons were almost totally lacking, but I have never had more appreciative guests.

While Mata'aisi and I were getting the people fed, Farquhar had been checking the house to see how it was withstanding the storm.

His report was alarming. Our bedroom, as we already knew was gone. So was the garden school house down in front and Farquhar's work house in the back. The boat, which earlier in the day, we had seen playing leapfrog on the beach with another boat, had disappeared completely. Worst of all, the living-room wall with its big picture window was threatening to collapse. If it went, the whole house would follow and all of us, our family and villagers alike would be left without shelter. Fortunately Farquhar had a plan for saving the room. He found the flashlight and sent some men scouting beneath the house. When they came up, they were carrying three long four-by-sixes. One was put down half-way across the living room floor and nailed into place to be used as a back stop for the other two which were leaned against the front wall, one on either side of the big window, to act as braces. Against them relays of men leaned all night. Matching their strength and their will against the wind, they saved the house for us all.

When the day's darkness thickened into total blackness, we all prepared for the night. In the kitchen sat two groups of men who were determined that whatever happened the storm should not take them by surprise. By the light of a flickering lamp, they sat playing cards and cracking jokes. By their side they had a small portable radio that ground out an endless cacophony of island music distorted by static and punctuated at intervals by the latest storm warnings from Fiji. Behind the men, leaning against the walls sat women who now burst into a spate of conversation and now bowed their heads to watch the children who lay sleeping across their broad laps. In the dining-room and all down the halls bodies were overlapping one another, oblivious to the storm, limp in sleep.

As our bedroom had vanished, Farquhar and the girls and I moved into the guest room. We did not have to feel guilty at having quarters so much more spacious than anyone else's, nor was anyone tempted to share them with us as we were on the now exposed front of the house where every fresh blast of wind rattled the windows and shook the walls until the whole room seemed to spin in violent motion. Pushing the twin beds together to make one big bed, we put the girls between us so that, by bending our legs up in front of them, we could make a sort of shelter to protect them in case some flying thing shattered the windows and sent bits of broken glass raining down. Tami and Tupou were nine years old then—a wonderful trusting age. Feeling as they nestled against us a sense of security which we ourselves could not share and exhausted by the events of the day, they soon fell fast asleep. For us, it was a time of wakeful weariness.

Often we had scoffed at the Tongan fear of the dark, but that night we lit a lamp, turned it low and put it in a corner where it would be safe from the wind. Its wavering yellow light was like a friendly hand holding back the fearsome dark night. Fully-dressed, we lay listening to the storm which fell into a strange pattern of lull during which there was almost complete silence, followed by a distant roar that seemed to begin far down the harbour like some great monster gathering up its forces as it sped ever faster toward us until, with a mighty burst it flung itself against the house and exploded into noise. Once there was a sound as if some giant hand were tearing paper. The roofing iron was being ripped off the veranda leaving us in the front room more than ever exposed to the fury outside.

Yet that night finished, as all nights do, and we climbed stiffly out of bed to face a grey morning that brought no relief. Although we did not know it then, we had a second night of unabated storm to endure. The barometer fell to 27.365 and the full force of the hurricane beat upon us for forty hours. Sometimes when it howled like all the lost souls let out of hell, it was all we could do to keep ourselves from screaming back at it. No doubt the fact that the girls regarded us as their only security and that all our villagers were relying on us, was a steadying influence.

We had many people beside ourselves and our immediate enlarged household to think of. We were concerned about the Sisters in Neiafu because their convent stood on a high rise of land overlooking the harbour where it would be exposed to every wind. We feared for our Scotch friend, Dugald, captain of the government ship, *Hifofua*. We had heard on the radio that he had been on his way from Nuku'alofa to Vava'u when he got the first hurricane warnings. He had gone into Ha'apai, the middle island group, to dump his passengers and had then set out for the open sea where, with his crew, he proposed to ride out the storm. Since he had left Ha'apai, there had been no further word of him. Most especially we were worried about Tu'ifua. It seemed impossible that her old house with its shaky veranda should survive the storm.

With our fears and our worries, Thursday passed and sleepless

Thursday night and Friday and Friday night. When Saturday morning came, the wind still howled, but it was only wind. The hurricane had passed. Now when we looked out the windows, we saw, not the dark debris-filled murk of the past two days, but clear air and sunshine. The land was bare and so ugly it was painful to look at, but the harbour, though it was roughened with white capes, looked normal. When I noticed that a few boats had commenced to go up to Neiafu, I told Farquhar that I had better go to town and do some shopping. After all, our household was not geared to entertaining 143 guests and the food stock was getting very low.

"We have no boat for you to go in," he said sadly. He had already been down to the beach and come back holding in his hands a few shattered pieces of what had, a few short days before, been our boat.

"Never mind, I'll get Latu to take me in his canoe."

Latu had the biggest canoe in the village. Miraculously, it had come through the storm. Usually he could paddle it all the way across the harbour on the dry side of the waves, but there was no dry side to them that day. It takes the sea a long time to go down after a hurricane; so while Latu paddled, I bailed. In spite of my best efforts, we got very wet. We were half-way across to Neiafu when I happened to look back up the harbour. There I saw the *Hifofua* coming up at a great rate, splashing spray over her bow as she tore through the waves. "Hurrah," I shouted, "She's safe." Latu stopped paddling for a minute and looked back, too. When he again turned to face me his whole visage was lit by a smile. I knew that he was rejoicing as I was that people for whose lives we had feared, still lived.

As we reached the wharf, the *Hifofua* docked on the other side of it. By the time I had clambered out of the canoe onto the boat landing and run up the steps to the main wharf, she had come to anchor. In another minute Dugald, with his captain's cap set jauntily over one ear was running down the gangway. Generally speaking, we were two pretty undemonstrative people, but that day we hugged one another while over and over again we exchanged congratulations on both being alive.

"I thought a couple of times, we'd lost the ship," Dugald told me. "She damned near stood on her head in that sea." A big man and tall, he seemed even taller than ever as he added in a voice filled with pride, "But we managed to bring her through." Then, because he is a devout member of Scotland's Wee Free Church, he added soberly after a minute or two, "With God's help."

"Come on board," he invited, but now I knew he was safe, I was anxious to see how my other friends had fared. Bidding him goodbye, I went on my way. As I walked up the wharf and along the road, I heard from everyone I passed the words that were to come echoing through Vava'u for many a day, "*Malo mo'ui*," "thank you for being alive."

The Catholic church which, before the storm, had stood so proudly overlooking the harbour, was a mass of rubble. The Sisters' new schoolrooms were a pile of splintered sticks, the priest's house had been swept away, but the convent, a sturdy product of the twenties when buildings were made of good sound New Zealand kauri, had stood. With a sense of rejoicing, I hurried across the churchyard and was soon being welcomed into the convent by the white-robed nuns. When they had all thanked God for preserving me and had asked about Farquhar and the girls and how our house fared, the American Sister Annuncia, looked at me and asked in her practical way, "When did you eat last?"

"I don't know," I said and, indeed, I did not. Mata'aisi and I had been so busy seeing that all the household got fed that we had not found time to eat ourselves. "I thought as much," she said and turning aside, whispered to young Sister Fabienne who scampered off to the kitchen. In a very few minutes breakfast was set before me. As I ate, Sister Annuncia sat beside me and told me how the Sisters and all the convent girls and a good many of their neighbours, too, had fled down into the convent cellars and there spent the days of the storm.

"Why did you do that?" I asked. "The building seems to have come through very well."

She laughed. "It's come to rest now, sure enough," she said "but you should have seen it during the storm. I had to go up to the top floor once because I suddenly remembered I'd left all our money up there. Going up those steps was like climbing a rope ladder and when I got to the top this old place was pulling at its foundations like a ship tugging at its moorings."

When I had finished my breakfast, I thanked the Sisters and asked if there were anything I could do for them. "Send the

Bishop a cable," Sister Annuncia said. " He's probably wondering if we're still alive."

On my way to the wireless station, I met Tu'ifua walking in the street with some friends. Breaking away from them, she ran up to me, threw her arms around me and kissed me again and again. Then, holding me at arm's length as if to inspect me and make sure I was whole, she exclaimed, " *Malo mo'ui* . . . thanks for being alive. And how is Tami?"

"How is Tami?" she asked, as if she had not just finished asking that very question. I told her that her namesake was her usual healthy self. Then she asked about Farquhar and Tupou and the house.

"And what of your family?" I asked in turn. They were all well and what was more surprising her house, rickety old place that it was, had stood through the storm. " Perhaps," she said with a laugh, " it couldn't be swept away. There were so many people inside holding it down." She, too, had had a houseful of neighbours whose own houses, even more flimsy than hers, had fallen down soon after the wind started.

She walked with me to the wireless station and waited while I sent off the cable to the Bishop in Nuku'alofa. When I told her I had to shop and was then going back to 'Utulei, she said at once, " I'll come with you." She waited until we were in the canoe and Latu had started to paddle home before she confessed, " I want to see for myself how Tami is."

When we got home, we all had a good meal and then while the storm continued to blow itself out, a much needed rest. The following day was Sunday. Early in the morning, Teau, our town officer, came to ask if the people could hold a church service in the living-room. We said, of course, that they could. Soon all the villagers had gathered there and the house was filled with the sound of their voices lifted in Thanksgiving. Their Wesleyan beliefs we do not share, but we shared with them their reverent sense of gratitude. Although all our houses and boats had been damaged or completely demolished, although we were all immeasurably poorer in material possessions than we had been before the storm, we felt a new luxuriant awareness of life and a sense of human comradeship that no storm could ever sweep away.

The following morning after breakfast, the people, polite as always, thanked Farquhar and me for keeping them and said that, after they had helped us clean up, they would go off to the village and start to rebuild their houses. We were glad they were such ideal guests, for the clean-up job was a major one. Buckets of mud that had been tracked through the rooms were collected by the women who then scrubbed the floors until they were clean and fresh. In the meantime, the men chopped and cleared away the trees and shrubs that had fallen in the garden, bailed out the well and generally got the place into some sort of order. The work outside was hard because the sun glared mercilessly down, with no protecting shade. The trees had lost all their branches, the coconut fronds had all fallen. Our whole world was as bare as if some mighty forest fire had burned through it—bare and glaring and unbelievably ugly—but we knew that the time of beauty would come again to Vava'u. We set to work to hasten the day.

CHAPTER NINETEEN

HILI AFA

Perhaps it is not surprising that for months after the storm whenever two Vava'u people met, the whole conversation was about the hurricane. There were some wonderful tales of things that happened—and, as time went on, some equally wonderful ones of things that never happened at all. One of my own favourites happened, but not until a week or so after the storm.

Among our hurricane "house guests" was Eleni. I felt sorry for her because the little house which she and her husband had built and the few possessions they had managed to gather in the first year of their marriage had all been swept away early in the storm. At any time, a big, awkward, raw-boned girl, Eleni was then enormous, swollen with pregnancy. During the first two days when the storm was raging she sat huddled against the kitchen wall moaning to herself. I paid no more attention to her than I did to anyone else, simply because there was not then time for private concern, but when Saturday came and we knew the storm had passed, I cleared the broken glass out of Tupou's room, made up the bed with fresh sheets and moved Eleni and her mother in.

She lay on the bed in the only dress she had—a cheap chartreuse chiffon with foot-wide bunches of scarlet roses scattered over it. It seemed to me, watching her, that the bunch over her belly quivered and spread with a life of its own. I asked her when the baby was due and she answered, as would any other villager, that she didn't know.

"Are you all right?" I asked then. Her mother, a thin, grey woman who had borne thirteen children of her own, said in a toneless voice, "She's all right."

I would have been reassured had not Eleni at that moment clasped the quivering bunch of roses and given forth a long crescent moan, " Oi . . . au . . . e, Oi . . . au . . . e". The sound of it sent me running across the house for Farquhar. He was lying on the bed in the guest room sound asleep, but I managed to shake him awake. " Come at once! Eleni's having her baby."

He rubbed the sleep out of his eyes and went across to where Eleni lay, but he was back in a remarkably short time.

" What's the trouble?" I asked.

" No trouble," he grunted.

" She's having the baby?"

He sighed. " Oh yes, sometime, but not now," and he plopped down on the bed and very determinedly shut his eyes and went back to sleep.

I could not forget Eleni's anguished moan. Before long the memory of it had drawn me back to her room. She was exchanging village gossip with her mother when I went in and seemed in good spirits. I felt a keen sense of relief, but . . . alas! it was short-lived. Soon the belly stretched roses started to quiver again. She gasped and " *Teu mate* . . . I'll die," she screamed at the top of her voice. Her mother, sitting on the floor beside her, did not move. Poor woman, I thought. She has been worn out by life, and again I went for Farquhar.

" What's it now?" he asked when I had again shaken him awake.

" Eleni . . . you must go."

He went. When he came back, he glared at me, but said nothing.

" You have no feelings," I accused him.

" And you," he retorted, " have no knowledge."

When I went to awaken him the third time, he said sleepily, " It's no use. I won't get up. I must get some sleep," and back to sleep he went at once.

On Monday when the people announced their intention of going up to the village and rebuilding their houses. Eleni's husband said he had already made a shelter for her, but I said to Farquhar, " We can't let that poor girl go up to the village."

" Why ever not?" he asked.

" The hill is so steep," I said. " She might have the baby half way up."

" Once and for all," he said with more patience than he felt, " she's not going to have that baby today or tomorrow. She probably won't have it for another week—maybe two. Eleni likes

(*right*) The 'Utulei town officer, Teau, speaking at a village feast. Tami, Tu'ifua and Farquhar in foreground. (*below*) Tupou and Tami dancing at a village celebration, 1968

In the wake of the hurricane: *(left)* In the wrecked school-house, Tami is holding the remains of our boat. *(below)* 'Utulei village with our house in the foreground

to yell. Lots of people do, but it doesn't mean a thing. She's perfectly all right."

So Eleni went up the hill. Farquhar's professional opinion was vindicated when, ten days after she went home, Eleni produced her first son. As I had been so concerned about his entry into the world, I was given the honour of naming him.

Queen Salote, exercising her prerogative, not as queen, but, as head of her own family, used to name all her young relatives. Most often she called them after what her elder son, the present king, was doing at the time. That practice resulted in a whole series of names that I used to laugh at. " Fishing at night," " Kava party," " Diving into Mariner's Cave." There was even one unfortunate little royal cousin who was christened, " Flying Through the Air to Britain on a Mission of Friendship!"

When, however, it fell to me to name Eleni's child, I did no better. I called him, " After the storm, a good clearing." I can only offer belated apologies for laughing at the queen's names and say that they, like mine, sound better in Tongan. Even so, " *Hili afa afu'a lelei,*" is quite a mouthful. Fortunately, the villagers have clipped it so that today Eleni's son is called simply " After the storm . . . *Hili afa.*"

CHAPTER TWENTY

TAPA DE COTY

When the sea settled down after the hurricane, one of the inter-island ships picked up the passengers that Dugald had left at Ha'apai and brought them on. The Captain told me that as soon as they sighted the first of the islands of Vava'u, they got up and stood at the railings so they could see what had happened to their homeland. But for the familiar shapes of the islands, nothing at all was recognisable. Gone was the verdant tangle of the bush lands, gone the waving fronds of the coconuts, gone even the slightest hint of green. The land was brown and bare in the glare of the shadowless sun. The gay line of villages that once dotted the beaches was nothing but heaps of broken timber and shattered glass. The Captain said, " As the ship passed slowly up the harbour, they stood silent. Never a word did they say, but the tears streamed down their cheeks until it broke your heart to see them."

We who were here understood exactly how those returning Vava'u men and women felt. The ugliness of the land was a pain that assaulted our eyes and tore at our hearts, but there were no tears in 'Utulei. There was far too much to do to allow time for weeping. First, there was a search. Each man tried to find the bits of timber and iron that had been his home and when he had found them, he had to patch the poor broken bits together so that his family could have shelter. He had, too, to clear the bush lands and plant anew. So much was there to be done, that the people scarcely knew where to start.

Although between 90 and 97 per cent of all housing in the Vava'u group had been destroyed, there were miraculously few injuries and only two deaths. In Neiafu, many people sheltered in the Wesleyan church. When the walls began to sway, everyone ran out, but the steward, remembering that the big church Bible had been left behind, went back to get it and was crushed to death by the collapsing walls. A woman in an outer village died when she was pinned beneath her falling house. Had it not been that the storm began in the morning hours, there would have been many more casualties. As it was, most people had found, during the hours of light, a safe place to shelter. Here in 'Utulei, all of our 143 "guests" were in the house by noon of the first day.

Before the days of quick communication and transportation which have made it possible for food and drugs to reach a stricken area in a matter of days, the suffering caused by such a storm must have been great. Then the quick deaths would have been the happy ones. Many of the very old, the young, and the weak must have known the horror of slow death from starvation.

The people were more fortunate after our hurricane. Help came with the first boat and even before that the stores had supplies which those who had money could buy and the churches and the few *papalangi* homes had tinned food that could be shared with neighbours. No one was in any danger of immediate starvation, but we realised that it would be a long time before Vava'u could again be self-supporting. In the meantime, the people would need all the help they could get.

For several years, my friend Sister Annuncia, had been corresponding with Tom Dooley, the famous young American doctor who, by his example, led so many young people into a life of service for others. Just before the hurricane, she lent me one of his books, an autographed copy that she greatly prized. Unfortunately, I had been reading it in bed and when our bedroom roof was whipped off, the wind picked it up and tore it to shreds. Yet, though physically it was destroyed, the book had a continuing power for good. When I knew that the storm had ruined all the food crops and foresaw hungry days ahead for our village people, I remembered reading in it of the great help that the Meals-For-Millions people had given Dooley for his starving Laotians.

Meals-For-Millions is the result of one man's compassion for his fellow men. The man, Clifton Clinton, ran a string of cafeterias in the Los Angeles area during the depression years. He specialised in serving good meals cheap. While other eating places were closing their doors through lack of customers, his were making a fortune. When it was made, Clinton's thoughts turned, not to the luxuries it might have brought him, but to the millions of people all over the world who had never known what it was to have a good meal. Determining to feed them, he hired scientists and told them his plan. In time they developed what today is known as "MPF," multiple purpose food. Looking like dark corn meal, it can be manufactured very cheaply from parts of grains and cereals which are usually thrown away in the process of refinement. It keeps well under any conditions and a couple of tablespoons a day will supply all the necessary food values.

I had, just after the hurricane, fifty dollars which I had been saving to buy some much-wanted books. Half of it, I sent off to the Meals-For-Millions people, explaining what had happened to Vava'u. With the other half, I bought milk powder which we began at once to give out to all the 'Utulei families that had babies or small children. Then I sat down and wrote letters to all my friends in America and asked them to help me keep our village fed. Their response was immediate. Every mail brought a shower of checks that, when they were all added up, enabled us to keep the entire village in milk and MPF for as long as it needed help which turned out to be for about a year.

When the first shipment of MPF came through, I found that not only had they sent twice as much as I had paid for, but they asked if we could not also use some for the hospital. The shipments which they subsequently sent were a great help. Patients in Vava'u are not fed by the hospital, but by attendants from their own families who come with them and remain as long as they stay, bringing food from home and cooking it in kitchens on the hospital grounds. Without the MPF which the nurses distributed to the attendants most of them would have had little to cook and many cases would have been complicated by malnutrition.

Here in 'Utulei, I saved the tins in which powdered milk came and issued two to each household. Once a week, all the tins were brought down to our kitchen where they were filled with MPF and milk powder. As Tami and Tupou and their village playmates were at the age at which filling tins and delivering them back to the village was great fun, the job of distribution was quickly and happily done. While they were doing it, they learned more about loving their neighbours than they could have done from listening to a hundred sermons.

By the time a year and a half had gone by, the beauty of Vava'u had returned and the land once more poured forth its fruits. The vegetation which had been destroyed in the storm covered the land with a thick mulch in which all the Tongan vegetables grew as they had never done before and *papalangi* vegetables such as tomatoes, cucumbers, corn and beans which the people planted for the first time, flourished, too. As if to rival the vegetable kingdom, animals, too, knew increased fertility and pigs and chickens abounded on land and the sea was full of fish. Food was everywhere, but cash was scarce. The reason for that was that Vava'u's two money crops—coconuts and bananas were not producing. The hurricane had blown all the bananas down. Normally new shoots would have come on and been bearing by the following year, but a deadly fungus disease attacked the plants. Agricultural scientists had no cure for it and it was many years before Vava'u again began to ship bananas. Even now, ten years later, these islands have not reached their pre-hurricane production.

So many coconut trees had been topped by the storm that much of the bush resembled the bombed plantations I had seen in New Guinea during World War II. Those trees never recovered. They had to be replaced. For a coconut to grow from seed to bearing requires ten years so, even had the people been able to replant at once, nuts would have brought no speedy solution to their problems. As a matter of fact, few people were able to replant immediately after the storm. Most of them were forced to use what nuts they had for food. All of those trees that were not killed outright were damaged—their fronds broken and the fruit and flowers blown off. Regeneration of the damaged trees was a slow business stretching out over as much as two or three years.

So it happened that the people were rich and poor at the same time. They had had a hard time rebuilding for much of the timber and roofing iron of which their homes had been made had been swept into the sea and it was hard to find even enough cash to buy nails to put together the pieces that were left. Still, every man in 'Utulei had managed to provide some sort of shelter for his family. The women had woven new sleeping mats and helped the men clear the bush lands. Even the smallest children had been working to help get Vava'u back to normal.

One thing all of us—villagers and our household, felt in great need of, was a holiday. It was provided for us when, in April, Farquhar's brother, Willie and our Sydney friends, Barney and Vera Greer, came to visit us.

Willie, the bachelor uncle of the Matheson clan, had visited us six or seven times before and had long ago established a warm avuncular relationship with the whole village. At kava parties he had advice and tobacco for the men and on picnics, a winning smile for the women and candy for the children. On that first trip after the hurricane, he won every feminine heart in the village by bringing in his great leather suitcase a dress-length for each woman. As they had all been garbed in second-hand relief clothes which had the peculiarity of never fitting anyone, Uncle Willie's gift was the occasion of great rejoicing.

The day after he and the Greers arrived, the village women came down to meet them and to bring food presents—baskets of papayas and oranges, big yams and a chicken or two with their feet tied firmly together. When the presentation had been made, the women began to talk to Willie, picking up again the old jokes they had enjoyed on his last visit.

Before very long, they were laughing and talking with the Greers, too. By occupation an advertising man, Barney, tall, thin, redheaded, has an artist's sensitivity and a mobile face that crinkles often into an understanding smile. His pretty Vera, gifted artistically and musically, is the gentle sort of woman that Tongans find it easy to love.

Looking back on the time when the three of them were here, it seems to have been a month of perpetual feasting. The village people were rich and poor all at once. They had no money, but they had an abundance of pigs, chickens, fish, yams, taro—indeed of all the good things to eat which the land and the sea provide. Willie and Barney and Vera stayed with us, but they were guests of the whole village and in their honour there were endless celebrations. The week they arrived, there was a welcome feast with the *polas*—the long stretcher-like tray tables made of woven coconut fronds, piled high with food. A few days before they left, there was a farewell feast and in between the two, whenever there was the slightest excuse, there was a feast or a picnic.

Our three guests were overwhelmed by the richness of the land and by the kindness of the people, but being perceptive individuals, they understood when they walked up in the village and looked at the small houses put together from scraps picked up after the hurricane and at the torn ragged clothing which everyone wore, that beneath the abundance, was want. The bushlands fed them, but no matter how simply a Tongan family lived, there were still things for which they needed money—clothing, soap, kerosene, milk powder, school fees. Without money, none of those things was possible.

On a day when a cruise ship came to Vava'u, I invited our visitors to come over to Neiafu to see our village show.

"What kind of show?" they asked. I explained to them that I had talked the store manager who was the agent for the cruise ships into letting the women put on a little programme showing how *tapa* cloth was made and how mats and baskets were woven. "It gives them a bit of money," I said, "and the tourists really enjoy the show."

"We're tourists," Barney said. "Let's all go."

The others agreed and after breakfast when Farquhar went to the hospital, we all crossed over to Neiafu with him.

At the wharf lay the big cruise ship. It had brought festival to town. The streets, usually so empty and so quiet, were filled with tourists in their gay-coloured holiday clothes. They bought shell necklaces and loaded themselves with baskets and grass skirts hawked by smiling Tongans. They bumbled in and out of stores, took pictures of pretty Vava'u girls and got involved in conversations that used gesticulations and smiles in place of words.

We made our way to the post-office square where, under a big ovava tree, we found a group gathered around the little enclosure that our 'Utulei women had made for their show. They had set up printed English signs that I had made for them that described the process of making *tapa*. Beside the first was a freshly-cut sapling of the paper mulberry tree from whose bark the *tapa* cloth is made. Beneath the next sign, a woman skilfully stripped the bark from the tree in long thin pieces. Other women soaked it and still others pounded the softened bark against a hollow log, beating it out with a heavy wooden mallet, making as they did so the rhythmic drumming that is part of the daily music of Tonga. Further along, another group joined the strips together with paste made from manioc and still others applied to the big pieces of cloth, the traditional designs in soft browns and shining black.

It takes weeks to make a piece of *tapa*, but the show enabled the tourists to see the whole process. Further, it reminded them of something the white world often seems to have forgotten—that work can be a tremendous amount of fun. Each woman had a flower tucked into her hair and a sweet-smelling *lei* around her neck. Each had on her face a welcoming smile. As they worked and held up the *tapa* at various stages of its manufacture, they laughed and chattered softly among themselves or broke into a gay song. The tourists in general were loud in their appreciation and so were our three. Barney moved up and called to Amelia who was beating the bark into thin strips of cloth. " Let me see a piece of that newly beaten cloth."

Obligingly, she tossed him a long strip. He held it up to the light. " Look," he said, " You can see the grain of the wood in the cloth and here's a hole where a twig once grew." He held it against his cheek. " How soft it is," he said, " How smooth and how good and earthy it smells. It's wonderful stuff! "

When we got back to 'Utulei, Willie and Vera were talking of the women's singing, but Barney was still talking of *tapa*.

" There's only one thing wrong with their show," I said.

" What's that?" he asked.

" It's just that we get so few cruise ships that they can't do it often enough to make much money."

" Yes," Barney said slowly. " Yes."

When, a few days before they were due to leave, Barney told me that he and Vera would like to give the villagers a present to show their appreciation of the friendliness the 'Utulei people had shown them, we had a round table discussion of what would be suitable.

" Not food," Farquhar said. " They have plenty of that and we still have milk for the babies."

" Not kerosene," somebody said, " some of them don't have lamps."

" Then what about lamps?" Vera said.

I shook my head. " The stores are out of them."

" And out of most everything else, too," Tupou put in.

" What about laundry soap?" suggested Tu'ifua who had joined the discussion. " Every household needs it."

Vera frowned. " That doesn't seem like much of a present."

" Perhaps not," Tu'ifua agreed, " but when you can't afford to buy it yourself, it is a very nice present. If you don't like to give them laundry soap, what about toilet soap? Everyone needs that, too."

" Let's get both laundry soap and toilet soap," Barney said.

When next Farquhar went to town the Greers went with him, returning with cases of soap and, in addition, a bright coloured bath towel for every household.

The following day, I provided them with a big basket into which they put enough soap and towels for the houses along the beach. Carrying it between them, they set off. Almost at once, they were back with the basket more full than when they'd set out.

"Why didn't you tell us how it would be?" Vera demanded, holding up in one hand a beautiful shell necklace and in the other a finely woven basket. "The minute we gave them the towel and soap, they insisted on giving us these."

"I've never known such generous people," Barney said, "but we don't want them to give us things. They've already done so much for us."

"In that case," I said, "you'd better get the girls to finish your deliveries for you," and that is what they did.

"What a wonderful present for the village," Tu'ifua said, but Barney shook his head and said thoughtfully, "It's so little. I wish we could find a way to be a real help to them."

The Greers had not been back in Sydney very long before I received a letter from Barney. He asked if 'Utulei could make him 12,000 pieces of *tapa*. He explained that he had the Coty account for Australia and had decided to use tapa to promote a new line, "Tapa de Coty". The biggest piece he wanted was to be used as a backdrop for window displays and was to be two feet by four. Smaller pieces were to be used as mats for cosmetics to stand on, as banners and as covers for the dealers' books. He set down the prices he was prepared to pay. They added up to a sum that, in 'Utulei terms, was astronomical.

When I read his letter, I walked up the hill to the house of Ana, the chairman of the village women's committee. She was peeling yams for her evening meal when I arrived, but when I told her why I had come, she stopped at once.

"Perhaps you could call the women together tomorrow and I could explain to them just what Barney wants," I said.

Ana shook her head. "No. This is too important to wait until tomorrow. We'll come down to your house right after dinner tonight."

That night, when we had finished eating, Farquhar and the girls disappeared into the library and I prepared the living-room for the women's coming. Like all Polynesians, Tongans prefer the floor to chairs, so I pushed the chairs back against the wall making plenty of room for the people to sit on the big mat. Then, because the villagers always talk more easily when they have cigarettes to puff on in between times, I put ash trays down and got out a fresh box of their favourite Grey's tobacco and several packages of papers.

Not long after I had finished those preparations, I heard the women coming across the lawn and climbing the steps to the veranda. One by one they came into the living-room and sat down on the mat in a big circle. When they were all there, I gave Ana the box of tobacco, the papers and an old magazine. As always on such occasions, she first counted the women, then carefully tore out for each one a page of the magazine onto which she put a share of tobacco and the papers. When the division had been fairly made and each women had received her portion, there was a moment or two during which cigarettes were rolled, tamped and lighted.

While they were going through that most important process, I looked about the room. There was Tupou's beautiful slender mother, Soko, and her aunt, Priscilla and the calm Teu. There, too, was old Anaise and her sister, Takua with their necks tied up in the red scarves of the " angels," a select society of aged Wesleyan women. Next to them was the gay Fifita with a frangipani bloom lopped over one ear. Filling in the corner was jolly fat Luisa who once while going across to Neiafu with Farquhar laughed so heartily and so heavily at one of his jokes that the seat she was hee-hawing up and down on collapsed into the bottom of the boat. By her side was Aemilia and her mother, Folau, widows both, who live together and have the most beautiful of all village gardens. All the others were there, too—the serious old ones and the laughing young ones—people with whom we had shared so many of the small daily events that give life its flavour.

When their faces began to float in the smoky atmosphere, I knew they were ready for me to start. I got out Barney's letter and translated it to them, explaining as I went along what he wanted and how much he would pay. They had all, I knew, been worried about their children's school fees and now I could see, looking over the sheet from which I read, the smiles of relief settling over their faces. When I had finished, they said, all together, "Thank you and for your friend Barney," and "Thank you, Barney, for your love."

I let them talk on for awhile and then I said sternly. "Now, listen. Sometimes you make very nice *tapa* and sometimes it's not so good. Sometimes you are in a hurry and the designs are blurry or you spill dye and forget to wipe it off . . ."

They looked, each one at her neighbour. Their smiles faded, they hung their heads and Ana said, "What you say is right. Sometimes we do very bad work." She looked straight into my eyes and added, "but sometimes, we do very good work."

At that the women looked up again and the smiles returned to their faces.

"I know you can do good work," I said. "What I am telling you is that this is not just a piece of *tapa* to roll up and sleep in. This must be very good *tapa*. It is for Barney and for people all over Australia who will be looking at it."

"Io, fine'eiki," they chorused. "Yes, yes, we understand."

"And furthermore," I continued, "I must be the one to judge this *tapa*. If any of you makes a piece that is not good, you must make it over."

"Of course," they chorused again.

I tried then to explain why Barney wanted the cloth. Except for the beer and cigarette ads on ZCO, Tonga knows little of the great business of advertising. I am not sure they knew much more when I had finished, but they knew that Barney was ordering *tapa* from them and they would be able to pay their children's school fees with the money he sent for it. That was all they needed to know.

The circle of women grew closer together and they talked for awhile among themselves in rapid Tongan. When they had finished, Ana turned to me and said, "We will work in two groups—the beach people in one group and the hill people in the other. We will make two *lau nimas*." (A *lau nima* is about twenty feet wide and is as long as the old cricket pitch in front of the church).

"That is good," I said. I gave each woman a piece of paper on which I had written the measurements of the pieces Barney wanted. I would like them, I explained, to go away and try to draw on those papers suitable designs. I printed for them "Tapa de Coty" and told them that the lettering would have to appear on each piece.

They nodded and smiled and after a good deal more conversation and many thanks to me and to Barney, they left.

The next day, 'Utulei burst into activity. The men went to the bush and came back with loads of paper mulberry saplings and the women began at once to strip off the bark and put it to soak. In a few days all the hillside echoed with the sound of *tapa* beating.

Those early stages of the work proceeded smoothly, but when the women began to bring in the papers on which they had tried to make designs, I was filled with despair. The designs were excellent for pieces of *tapa* twenty feet wide where the natural tendency of the dyes to run and blur made little difference, but none of them was suitable for scaling down to the size of the pieces Barney wanted and not one of the women had succeeded in reproducing Coty's typical squat letters.

I called a meeting and again I told them what was needed. Again they smiled and said they understood, but when the papers came back, the designs were worse than ever.

"I guess we'll have to give the whole thing up," I said to Farquhar. "They just can't seem to get the idea."

"You can't give it up," he said soberly. "It means too much to the people." He was silent for a minute and then he said. "You'll just have to help them, that's all."

In the end, I drew a simple design of a hibiscus with a border of maile, the sweet smelling vine of which old time Tongans made wreaths for their heroes.

Generally the pattern is applied to *tapa* by means of a template fitted over a log. The raised portions of the template which are made of coconut mid-ribs are painted with the dye and the *tapa* is pressed against it. As such a method could not be adapted to the small-size pieces we were working on, we decided to try stencils. From the hospital, Farquhar brought home some old X-ray plates. I cleaned the chemicals off them with Clorox, chalked on my designs and cut them out to make the stencils.

I finished them just about the time the women finished the two big lengths of *tapa*. There was a long day spent in staining the pieces a light reddish brown that was to be the background colour. Then followed two days of cutting the necessary number of small pieces—two days which reduced every pair of scissors in the village and every razor blade to a state of useless dullness. When all that preliminary work was over, I gave out the stencils and explained their use. That much of the work was fairly automatic, but the final step was a difficult one. With a piece of rolled coconut husk for brush and the shiny black paint made of Tongan oil and candle nut soot, the design was outlined and the hibiscus completed by drawing its characteristic upstanding style with the five surrounding anthers.

With naïveté bordering on stupidity, I had always assumed that because *tapa*-making was a traditional Tongan craft, all Tongan women could turn out beautiful *tapa* cloth. That is simply not true. Everyone can strip the bark from the sapling and soak it and all can pound it out to the proper thickness, but when it comes to supplying the colour and outlining, there are only a few *nima potos*—clever hands. I was interested in observing that the few—about four women out of the whole village—who did the most careful finishing and outlining, were also the ones who were the most observant. Some of the women came up with polka-dotted flowers that looked more like Tiger lilies than hibiscus, some in an excess of enthusiasm drew a whole fuzzy bunch of stamens in place of the hibiscus' invariable five, and many in outlining "Tapa de Coty" forgot a letter or two in spite of the fact that the stencilled shape was plain for them to follow. The *nima potos*. however, turned the five stencilled petals into true and beautiful hibiscus with the exact number of stamens and the petal markings just as they appear on the blooms in the garden. After a few afternoons on which I rejected more pieces than I accepted, the women and I talked the matter over and decided to let the *nima potos* do all the outlining and finishing while the others worked full time on the preliminary steps. It was a wise decision.

About two weeks after they began working on designs, there was an afternoon when all the women came together and watched anxiously as I inspected the day's offerings piece by piece. As soon as I had accepted the last one, they gave a loud shout and running down onto the lawn began to dance and sing for joy. The long job was over.

In due time the *tapa* arrived in Sydney and soon we had Barney's cheque. It paid all the school fees that year and left each woman with a little extra to buy kerosene and other essentials from the store. How Australia responded to Tapa de Coty, I do not know, but there is one village in Vava'u where Coty is, indeed, a household word.

CHAPTER TWENTY-ONE

CHARLIE'S PRESENT

STANDING ON the wharf in Neiafu watching the *Laganbank* come alongside, I looked up to the bridge and spotted my old friend, Eloise, who was coming to spend three months with us.

" There she is," I said to Tami who stood by my side.

" Which one?" Tami asked, as we waved.

" The tall one," I replied, noticing then the dark-haired young woman up on the bridge next to my friend. It had been a long time since I had seen Eloise's family and I am unfortunately near-sighted so I said, " Perhaps the other one is her daughter."

My practical down to earth Tami said, " She wouldn't bring her without letting you know."

Tami was right. Nevertheless, when Eloise came down onto the wharf, the young woman was still with her. Very shortly she was introduced to us as Romola, an Australian whom Eloise had met in Nuku'alofa and with whom she had quickly struck up a warm friendship. We discovered that Romola had just earned an MA degree in anthropology from the University of Colorado and was having a leisurely look at the Pacific islands before going on home to take up an appointment in the University of Brisbane.

While Polito was getting Eloise's bags off the ship and into our boat, we all stood talking on the wharf. I expressed the hope that we would see something of Romola while she was in Vava'u.

" I'm sure you will," she replied, " because I'm going to be staying with a friend of yours."

" Oh," I said. " Who's that?"

" Tu'ifua."

To say the least, her words surprised me. At that very moment, Tu'ifua was in my kitchen in 'Utulei putting the finishing touches on what was to be Eloise's first breakfast with us. As usual, when we were getting ready for company, she had been with us for days helping me get the house and garden into order. It would, I well knew, have been quite impossible for her to be expecting a *papalangi* guest without so much as mentioning it. Being reasonably sure she had never even heard of Romola, I said, " Well, as a matter of fact, Tu'ifua is down at my house at the moment. Perhaps you'd better come to breakfast with us and meet her."

When she agreed, Polito put her case on top of Eloise's bags and we all squeezed into the boat for the trip across the harbour. It was the sort of morning we like to think of as typical Vava'u weather—crisp and sunny with the sea so calm and clear that you could stare down to the depths where electric-blue fish played in and out of lace-like coral and beyond that to where pink and yellow starfish lay like overstuffed sofa cushions on the sandy bottom.

When we reached 'Utulei, we found Tu'ifua and Tupou waiting on the beach to meet us. We all walked up to the house together and while I showed Eloise her room and took her around to the side veranda to meet Farquhar, Tu'ifua and Romola talked.

It was then that Tu'ifua learned that during the several weeks that Romola had spent in Nuku'alofa, she had met Tu'ifua's cousin, Charlie, who runs one of the movies down there. When he had learned of her interest in old Tonga, he took her out to see the Ha'amoga, the great stone trilithon which, looking like one unit of Stonehenge, has baffled countless anthropologists. He saw, too, that she got to the terrace tombs where ancient Tonga's kings were buried and to the sites of long-abandoned villages.

Because Charlie is a Vava'u man, it was inevitable that he was soon telling his new friend of the beauties of his home islands. Romola, catching his enthusiasm, asked how she could get to Vava'u and what sort of accommodation she would find there. With typical Tongan helpfulness, he assured her that his cousin, Tu'ifua, would be delighted to have her stay at her house and that he would arrange transportation.

When, a few days later, he told her everything was settled and that he had booked passage for her on the *Laganbank*, she quite naturally assumed that he had contacted his cousin. He could have done so by radio telephone or by cable, but such a thought never entered Charlie's head. A Tongan has as many homes as he has relatives. Naturally, he feels perfectly free to send his friends to any of them. He gave Romola a note of introduction to Tu'ifua and that, he felt was all that was necessary.

On that first morning, after I had left Eloise talking to Farquhar, I went into the living-room. The girls told me Romola was washing up for breakfast, so I went on into the kitchen to see that everything was in order for the meal. There I found Tu'ifua in tears. When I asked her what was the matter, she told me how Charlie had sent Romola to her. " I don't know why he did this to me," she sobbed. " It would be different if she were a Tongan, but my house is too full for a *papalangi* and I have no proper food for her."

I knew well that what she said was true. Her house in Neiafu, smaller than ours, was fairly bulging with the fourteen people who lived in it. So far as eating went, they managed very well on food from the bush, but they had little money to buy butter, milk, tinned fruits and all the other things that Tu'ifua felt were essential to *papalangis*.

" If only there were a hotel here in Vava'u," Tu'ifua said.

I nodded sympathetically, but I had no solution to offer. However, Tu'ifua had. " We'd better," she said, " leave her here."

" You can't," I said quickly. " Eloise has just arrived for three months and Farquhar is still recovering from his operation. It's all he can do to make it over to the hospital without having to put up with extra people."

Tu'ifua looked imploringly at me, her big eyes swimming with tears. As if I had forsaken her, she turned away and mournfully addressing the walls asked, " What am I going to do?"

There may be people who can withstand a flood of Polynesian tears. I am not one of them. " I don't know what to do about it," I said, " but I'll take her round to see Farquhar and we'll see what he says."

When I had explained the situation to Farquhar, I went and got Romola and, after introducing them, left them alone. In those days whenever Farquhar met young people who were not particularly attractive to him, he excused himself by saying, " They belong to a different generation. We have nothing in common. I can't understand them."

He made no such excuses about Romola. Was it because— although she comes from Perth, her forebears came from the Isle of Skye which is just across the water from the Matheson country?

(*right*) Farquhar and Felemi in the wreckage of our bedroom. (*below*) Mataisi, the schoolteacher, with Semisi, Lavinia's father, in what remained of his house. Although this is some distance up the hill from our house the contents of our bedroom were borne up here by the hurricane, and Lavinia's mother was returning things to us for days afterwards

(*left*) The author.
(*below*) Tami, Betty Buck and Tupou – in Boston

Or because with her dark curly hair, fair skin and bright eyes, she reminded him of the pretty Scotch girls of his youth? Or because he shared her interest in anthropology? Or because he liked the quick sense of humour that seemed to bubble up from the depths of her? I don't know, but when I went again to the veranda, I found them talking together like old friends after a long separation. Farquhar looked up at me and said, " Romola doesn't mind sharing the guest room with Eloise—so of course, she'll stay with us while she's in Vava'u."

" I will," she said shyly, " if you don't mind."

" I'll be delighted," I told her, feeling great relief that Tu'ifua's problem was so happily solved. " It will be wonderful having my oldest friend and my newest one both here at once."

My speech was not merely a hostess's polite rhetoric. We had all recognised Romola at once as one of us—a person who seemed to belong here in 'Utulei. She was, on that first day, a friend. So, in the years that have passed, she has remained.

She was with us then for ten days. Tu'ifua stayed, too, so we were a full household. During the day while Farquhar was at the hospital or resting at home, we took the boat and went up and down the harbour visiting as many islands as we could. The girls and I had been to them all before, but with Tu'ifua to tell the old tales over again, with Romola to make her keen observations and tell us how Tongan customs compared with those of the Navajos she had lived among during her stay in America, and with Eloise bringing fresh enthusiasm to everything, we saw all the old familiar places with fresh eyes.

In due time, Charlie received a wrathful letter from Tu'ifua and when next he visited Vava'u, we explained to him that when *papalangis* were involved, there were certain limitations to old Tongan hospitality. Our scoldings were softened by the fact that however much we deplored his failure to forewarn Tu'ifua, we also found it necessary to thank him for Romola who in 'Utulei is always known as "Charlie's present"!

CHAPTER TWENTY-TWO

QUEEN SALOTE TUPOU, 1900-1965

BECAUSE FARQUHAR was on the sick list on the morning of Wednesday, 16th December 1965 and was not able to go to the hospital, I decided to go across to Neiafu by myself to do some necessary shopping. I took the boat and set out on the ten-minute run across the harbour. The day was clear, sunny, still and as I approached the town the waterfront stores of Neiafu shone bright against the poster blue sky. I tied up at Morris Hedstrom's wharf and, beginning to walk up the path to the main store, thought to myself that it was, indeed, a perfect day. Then, suddenly, my glance fell on the white shaft of the flag pole at the head of the main wharf. The bright red and white flag of Tonga was not flying aloft as usual. Disconsolately, it drooped at half-mast. Up the hill I hurried and into the main street, but it was strangely empty. I crossed and went into Morris Hedstrom's store. Behind the counters, the clerks were red-eyed and silent. The manager came up and I looked at him and asked, " Is it . . .?"

He nodded, " Yes, she's gone." Tonga's great queen, Salote, was dead.

Her death was not unexpected. For over a year the dreaded word "cancer" had struck terror into Tongan hearts as they watched their beloved queen, once so active in everything that pertained to the kingdom or to the Wesleyan church, retiring gradually from public life. Whenever a ship came to Vava'u from Nuku'alofa the first question on everyone's lips had been, " How is she?" and when she had been seen out driving in the Royal car or enjoying the sun from the Palace veranda, the people had let themselves, as people will, believe that perhaps after all, she might get better. When, however, Parliament was opened and closed without her—she who had always stood so proudly in front of that great assembly, the time of pretence was passed. Kaloniuvalu, one of the three nobles who represented her in Parliament, read her closing speech to the assembly. In it she spoke of the elections that were due to be held before the next meeting and asked, "Who knows whether we will all be present next year?" It was a question that brought foreboding to all who heard it. The very month after Parliament was closed, she was flown to New Zealand in a special RAF plane made available to her by Queen Elizabeth. The doctors there helped relieve her pain, but it was too late for hope.

By the time I returned to 'Utulei, the people at home had already heard the news. Farquhar was lying on the couch in the library with the girls sitting beside him listening to the radio.

"She died just after one o'clock this morning," he told me and added, "She was surrounded, as she would have wished to be, by her own people. Her uncle, Lepa, and Prince Tu'ipelehake and his wife, Melenaite and their daughter, Fusipala . . ."

"And Tungi, the Crown Prince?" I asked; for I knew that, following a telephone message from his younger brother in Auckland he had prepared to fly to his mother's bedside.

Farquhar shook his head. "It is sad," he said. "He didn't reach Auckland until two o'clock, an hour after she had died." He turned to the girls, "You mustn't call him Tungi any longer. He is the King now."

On Friday, the *Chronicle*, the country's one newspaper, came out with heavy black edge that it was to carry during the six months of official mourning. There was a full page picture of the queen and over her head the banner headline. "*To ae la'a o Tonga*," the sun of Tonga has set. That is the old euphemism in which Tongans express the death of a ruler, but in Queen Salote's case, it had fresh truth. A general gloom settled over the country. During the mourning period no *tapa* was to be made, no guitars were to be played, no dances held. On ZCO, the only music to be heard was funeral dirges. Meanwhile, in New Zealand, the body of the queen lay in state while members of the Tongan community there filed sorrowfully by to pay their last respects.

The people here were proud of the honour New Zealand paid to the body of their queen, but they were not really content until it had been flown home and she was, in death, as she had been in life, with them. The coffin was placed in the royal chapel which stands in the palace grounds and there it lay in state until the funeral.

Around the events of ordinary life, the old Tongans built up a great amount of ceremony. Births, marriages, and deaths were the only events of their lives. Much of that ceremony still remains and nowhere is it in greater evidence than in a royal funeral.

To modern Europeans and Americans who hurry their dead into their graves and seldom go near them again, a Tongan funeral must seem a strange long-drawn-out affair, but when it is realised that the people look on it as their last earthly chance to express their love for the deceased, it begins to have more significance.

When word was received in Tonga of the Queen's death, the royal undertakers, an elite group whose position is hereditary, moved into the Palace grounds and started at once to work on the funeral arrangements.

The burial took place on 23rd December. Promptly at ten o'clock a party of Tonga Defence Force entered the royal chapel, lifted the coffin and carried it outside where it was placed on the bier which had been especially built. Its size may be judged by the fact that two hundred of Nuku'alofa's strongest men were required to carry it. In life, the queen had always been attended by her *matabules* and two of them mounted on the bier and sitting beside the coffin, accompanied her to the royal tomb. Nuku'alofa was crowded that day with all the people who had been able to get in to the capital, but everywhere in the Kingdom and all over the world wherever Tongans lived, people were, in spirit, following their queen's last procession.

Here in 'Utulei, Farquhar and the girls and I together with a group of neighbours, sat listening to the radio report.

" The procession is being formed now," Tami said and in another minute, the announcer was telling us that the guard of honour consisting of the Royal guard and one hundred members of the Tonga Defence Force, was leading off, followed by the Police Band.

The slow mournful notes of the death march filled Nuku'alofa and, going out over the air, the whole kingdom. " The royal bier is passing," said the announcer and the 'Utulei people who sat with us sobbed aloud.

The queen had been the fondest of grandmothers. It was particularly fitting that she was followed by her two eldest grandsons,

Crown Prince Taufa'ahau and Prince 'Uluvalu, who carried the insignia of her orders.

The rest of the Royal family followed and after them came rulers and representatives of foreign countries in many parts of the world. To Farquhar and me the list of foreign representatives, though it was certainly impressive, seemed of little interest, but to our Tongan neighbours each one was important because he represented the feeling of his country for the queen.

"The Governor of New Zealand, Sir Bernard and Lady Fergusson, representing Queen Elizabeth," said the announcer and old Ma'ata at my side wiped her streaming eyes and whispered, "Sir Bernard and Lady, thank you for your love."

"The Hon. Malietoa of Western Samoa," said the announcer and Ma'ata exclaimed, "*E malietoa*, thank you for coming."

The Governor of Fiji, Sir Derek and Lady Jakeway," said the announcer and "Sir Derek and Lady," echoed Ma'ata.

And so she went on until the last and lowliest of all the foreign representatives had fallen into line behind the slow-moving procession.

After them came the Ministers of the Crown, members of the European community and the general public. As the announcer told us of the last of the procession, we could hear the saluting battery of the Nuku'alofa waterfront firing the twenty-one gun salute. We heard it often enough in the past, on the Queen's birthday or when she left the country or returned to it, and always before it had had a fine, festive sound, but that morning it was twenty-one sharp, sad farewells.

When the party reached the royal tombs, the Queen's bier was rested on the tomb of her husband, Prince Tungi Mailefihi. The service itself was conducted by a group of Wesleyan ministers. When they had finished, the royal undertakers ordered a chosen group of black-clad Tongans, wearing big mourning mats to stand around the open grave with their backs to it, holding up tapa and fine mats to make a great screen around it. According to old Tongan custom only the undertaker is entitled to go into the grave and to see that the coffin is correctly placed in it.

When the burial had been completed and the last prayers had been said, the funeral was over so far as the foreign visitors were concerned. To the Tongans it was just beginning.

On the following day, the King, as head of his family, held the *pongipongi*. This old ceremonial consists to the eyes of an outsider mainly in the presentation of food and kava. It is much more than that. In the old days, before Europeans came and gave Tongans a written language, it was a time to review family history and, by a careful selection of the young people who were called upon to pick up the food gifts, introduce to the community at large, the members of the family of the deceased. Today we can read Tongan history in books, and ZCO and the weekly *Chronicle* keep a public which, like the English public, is sentimental about the lives of its rulers, fully informed on royal doings, but the *pongipongi* is as important a ceremonial as ever, probably because it fulfills not only the old practical need of establishing the position of the younger generation in society, but the continuing emotional need of talking out a farewell.

In the early days of European contact, the Protestant missionaries did their best to starve out the first Catholic priests and in the case of a few unfortunate French fathers, very nearly succeeded, but modern Tongans are true ecumenicals. Officially the country is Wesleyan. Queen Salote first became known to the outside world as the smiling queen of Queen Elizabeth's coronation, but as the devout queen who was an active church worker. She was, however, a friend of all churches. The priests and nuns who come to Tonga are an educated group whose gentle manners have been a great force of good in the community. The royal grandchildren have gone to the convent for lessons in piano, sewing, and French. It was only natural that the Catholic community honoured the queen in a great memorial mass held in January at the Cathedral in Nuku'alofa. Conducted by the very Rev. John Rogers, Bishop of Tonga, it was attended by the King and Queen and other members of the royal family and by a large group of local people.

In February, the King went to the volcanic island of Tofua to collect *kilikili*, the round black volcanic pebbles with which Tongans decorate graves. These stones continue to serve their original purpose of differentiating one grave from another for even today few Tongans raise headstones over the graves of their dead. Tofua which is famous in history as the site of the mutiny on the Bounty is surrounded by very rough waters. Nevertheless, the King and his party succeeded in collecting a whole boatload of the prized black pebbles which he took back to Nuku'alofa and gave into the keeping of the royal undertakers.

In April was held another great celebration, the Faka-po-Teau, or the celebration held a hundred nights after the queen's death. Led by the nobles of the Kingdom, a vast gathering of people filed into the Palace grounds bearing kava roots, pigs and baskets of shell fish. Following this ceremony, the mourners took off the largest roughest of the mourning mats and for the remainder of the mourning period wore smaller mats.

All these events were reported for us here in Vava'u by ZCO and by the *Chronicle,* but fortunately these modern means of communication have not done away with the older more personal means of disseminating news. Every boat that came brought travellers from Nuku'alofa. In the markets, at *kava* circles, whereever a group of people met, the travellers told of the wonders of the goings on in Nuku'alofa.

It was, however, not only in the capital that the funeral celebrations engaged the attention of the people. Here in Vava'u hundreds of women and children combed the beaches for the shining dark shells of native oysters or bright yellow cowrie shells. They were collected and cleaned and then, painstakingly, each one was pierced so that it could be strung. The sea was full of packages of *fau,* the wild hibiscus from which is made the raffia-like fibre that is used in making grass skirts, curtains, and grave hangings. The hangings were great woven curtains twelve feet wide and twenty or more feet long. Basically, they were woven of *fau* in all the intricate patterns of native basketry. Threaded on them, outlining the designs were the many shells. I think few foreigners, viewing these decorations, realise the tremendous amount of work that goes into them and fewer still are aware of the fact that each shell threaded into them represents the love of the common people.

Early in April when the hangings had been finished, they were strung for a few days along the veranda of the post office so all could see them. Meanwhile pigs, kava and other ceremonial foods were collected. Tu'ifua worked on all of these preparations and she went with the Vava'u people who on 15th April walked to the Palace and made a formal presentation to the King.

On the fourth of June, the final funeral ceremony was held. At four o'clock in the morning, the royal undertakers began to wash the *kilikili* pebbles which, in February, the King had brought from Tofua, in sea water poured into a special ceremonial bowl called the *scene*. As each lot of stones was washed, it was spread out on a bed of *tapa* cloth and mats under a specially constructed shelter and thoroughly dried. Then they were oiled with fragrantly scented Tongan oils and placed in small baskets which were passed along a living chain, formed by the men of the undertakers' families, until they reached the royal graveside. There they were spread over the grave by the Chief Undertaker. After the last of the stones was in place on the grave, the undertaker reported to the King. Their task was finished. At the Palace, they were formally thanked and given a food presentation after which for the first time in six months, they returned to their own homes.

The next day the period of mourning was officially over and on the day following the Princess Fusipala and Prince Aho'eitu, attended by a large group of women in the palace grounds, performed the *Tuki Putu*, the ceremonial beating of *tapa* which from earliest Tongan times, had announced to all hearers that the time of mourning was over and that the people could once more take up their normal lives, once again fill their villages with the sounds of work and the sounds of joy. Their grief at the loss of their queen was over, but their pride in her would never die.

CHAPTER TWENTY-THREE

THE END OF HANDSOME MEN IN TONGA

Queen Salote loved the stories of old Tonga which from time immemorial the old people had told in the long warm tropic nights to the children who gathered about them. Among my own favourites is this one which tells how the old gods of Tonga swore they would make no more handsome men.

Once upon a time a strange canoe landed on the beach near where there lived a large family of brothers. As soon as the eldest brother saw the visitors, he called the others and told them to collect food and dig a pit for an *'umu*, an earth oven, so that they could prepare a meal for the newcomers.

The younger brother, a frail sort of fellow, was sent to the bush to collect leaves with which to cover the *'umu*. Although he was suffering from sore feet, he set off willingly enough and gathered a great armful of leaves. As he was on his way back home three gods happened to see him. At once they took pity on him. He was so tired! He was so weak! He was not at all what a strong young Tongan should be!

" Hmm," said the first god, " whoever made him certainly made a mistake."

" I'm sure I never did such a poor job when I was making men," said the second god who was always on the defensive.

The third god who was the oldest of them all thought for a minute. Then he said, " I know what we will do. We'll refashion him."

He had no sooner spoken than he sprang up into a nearby tree so he could supervise the job. The other two seized Young Brother and chopped him up. They laid his arms, his legs, his hands, his feet—and all the other parts of his body carefully on the ground so that the old god up in the tree could see them plainly. When they were all laid out in order, the old god said, "Fix those feet. A man's feet should be strong to carry him many miles. His toes should be supple so he can pick things up with them or clasp the trunk of a coconut tree when he climbs after a nut."

The two gods did as they were told and when the feet were finished, they set them firmly on the ground.

"Just look at this thing," said one of the gods, holding up a leg. "Too short."

The second god held up the other leg and said, "It has no muscles at all."

So they stretched the legs out and put into them a new set of muscles that were as hard as the wood of the toa tree and as quick to move as the little eel that flashes through the coral at low tide and they covered them over with golden brown skin that was sun-proof and wind-proof and water-proof. And when they were finished, they fastened them carefully to the feet.

So they remade Young Brother bit by bit until he stood before them, a strong handsome young man, but the gods are hard to please. One found this wrong with him and one that, so in the end, they chopped him up once more and started all over again.

Three times they rebuilt him before they were satisfied. Then they gave him his bunch of leaves and sent him on his way.

Young Brother felt stronger and happier than he had ever felt in his life, but he did not know what a handsome fellow he had become until he leaned over a little forest pool and looked at himself in it. What he saw made him smile all the way from his face right in to his heart. The people still call the pool he looked into "Smiling Heart".

When he got home, the visitors smiled at him, too, but his brothers did not smile. At first they did not even recognise him, but when he handed them the leaves for the *'umu,* they knew that he was Young Brother. When he had been frail and had suffered from sore feet, his brothers had mistreated him because they knew he was too weak to protect himself. Now that he was so strong, they were afraid of him and out of their fear grew jealousy. Of all the evil feelings that darken men's hearts, jealousy is the most evil. So great did it grow in the heart of the oldest brother that he rose up when night had come and killed Young Brother as he lay sleeping.

When the three gods heard what had happened their wrath was

so great that they swore they would never again make a handsome man.

I think the Tongan gods must be like the Tongan people—quick to anger, but quicker still to relent; for, relent they certainly did. How do I know? I watch the young men of the village as they run up and down the beach for football practice. I see, Polito, my yardboy, climb high into the flamboyant tree and walk along its branches as if they were garden paths. I look into smiling brown faces that shine with good spirits and good health. I live in 'Utulei where all the young men are so strong and so handsome they could have been modelled after that unfortunate Young Brother.

CHAPTER TWENTY-FOUR

THE CAVE

Lord Byron, the famous English poet, and I have in common a point of failure—and that point is one of the most beautiful of all places in Vava'u. It is a cave located far down the harbour on the island of Nuapapu on a coast where the rocky undercut cliffs are so rugged that one trembles to think of ships passing anywhere near. Certainly the old wooden vessels of the early explorers, had they been driven onto it by unfavourable winds, would have been smashed to bits and the sailors, thinking to swim to a friendly shore, would have been impaled on the knife-sharp rocks and there met a fearsome death unless some miracle had led them to the cave . . . and miracle it would have had to be because the only way to get into that cave is by diving.

On calm days the entrance glows, a luminescent circle of azure set in the cobalt waves. If you dive eight feet down through the very centre of that bright circle, you will find a tube-like passage opening up in the coral. Swim about fourteen feet along that submarine way, but be careful not to yield to the temptation to look up at the coral ceiling. Beautiful it is, but treacherous, made up of a myriad needle like spikelets that hang mere inches above your head. Swim with your head down, with eyes shut, if you like. It does not matter. The end of the passage is unmistakable. A surge of water lifts you and effortlessly you are floated into the great chamber of the cave. It is such a place as some old Tongan sea-god might have created for his private retreat. The watery floor through which you swim gleams with a pale light reflected from the sands on the bottom of the cavern while forty feet above your head, the ceiling is vaulted in shadowy stalactites. When you weary of swimming, climb up on to the great rocky platform which stretches just above water level along one side of the room.

Here you have left the familiar earth behind you. Here is neither tree nor shrub, neither flower nor fern. There is only form and colour and primal light and darkness. And suddenly, even as you look at it, the whole place dissolves in a shimmering green gold mist. Born of sea surge, the mist is everywhere so thick that you can scarcely see your hand before your face. Then, as suddenly as it came, it goes. The air clears and again the cathedral-like chamber is around you. Yet a minute and the mists return and reality has again faded away in a dancing green light. When at last, it is time for you to return to the world, the trip is easy. You have only to sink into the floor and follow the light. Soon you will rise into the open sea beside the rocky cliff.

Why do I say the cave represents a failure to me? Why simply because, although I have been there a thousand times in my imagination, I have never been there in fact. But my description of it? Well, I have read Mariner's account of it and I have listened to white people and brown who have been in, but never have I seen more of it than the beautiful shimmering blue circle that marks its entrance.

Although I am a strong swimmer, I am a poor diver. To write, " Sink eight feet into the sea and swim about fourteen feet along a watery passage," is simple. To do it is, for me, impossible. It is true that a few people who dive no better than I do have managed to see the inside of the cave. They went in clinging ignominiously to a knotted rope pulled by a native guide. I would gladly have submitted to such a humiliating entry were it not that from the first time we ever went to the entrance of the cave, Farquhar raised violent objections to my going in. He told me of a young officer from a copra boat who, while trying to swim in, cracked his skull on the roof of the passageway and died. Having told me that unfortunate incident, he imagined that the matter was closed. Alas! He little realised what an irrational creature he had married.

Not long after that first trip to the cave entrance, we acquired our copy of Mariner and I read there how young Mariner, swimming off Nuapapu with his patron, Finau, was surprised when said, " I'm tired of swimming. Let's go and drink kava." Thinking that they would get back into their canoes and paddle around to some spot that offered a better landing, Mariner asked Finau where they would go.

"Follow me," the chief said and plunged at once into the depths of the sea. Without a question, Mariner went after him and, as he wrote, " guided by the light of his heels," followed him into the cave. All Finau's followers came after them and soon the great chamber was turned into a place of merriment. They lit flares, they made kava, and Mariner probably the first white man to behold it, marvelled at the cave which today bears his name.

Long before he saw it, the place was old in Tongan story, but let him tell the romantic tale in his own words:

" In former times there lived a *tooi* (governor) of Vava'u who exercised a very tyrannical deportment towards his people. At length when it was no longer to be borne a certain chief meditated a plan of insurrection, and was resolved to free his countrymen from such odious slavery, or to be sacrificed himself in the attempt. Being however, treacherously deceived by one of his own party, the tyrant became acquainted with his plan, and immediately had him arrested. He was condemned to be taken out to sea and drowned, and all his family and relations were ordered to be massacred, that none of his race might remain. One of his daughters, a beautiful girl, young and interesting, had been reserved to be the wife of a chief of considerable rank, and she also would have sunk, the victim of the merciless destroyer, had it not been for the generous exertions of another young chief who, a short time before, had discovered the cavern. This discovery he had kept within his breast a profound secret, reserving it as a place of retreat for himself, in case he should he unsuccessful in a plan of revolt which he also had in view. He had long been enamoured of this beautiful maiden, but had never dared to make her acquainted with the soft emotions of his heart, knowing that she was betrothed to a chief of higher rank and greater power. But now the dreadful moment arrived when she was about to be cruelly sacrificed to the rancour of a man, to whom he was a most deadly enemy. No time was to be lost; he flew to her abode; communicated in a few short words the decree of the tyrant; declared himself her deliverer, if she would trust to his honour, and, with eyes speaking the most tender affections, he waited with breathless expectation for an answer. Soon her consenting hand was clasped in his. The shades of evening favoured their escape; whilst the wood, the covert, or the grove, afforded her concealment. till her lover had brought a small canoe to a lonely part of the beach. In this they speedily embarked, and as he paddled her across the smooth wave, he related the discovery of the cavern destined to be her asylum till an opportunity offered of conveying her to the Fiji Islands. She, who had intrusted her personal safety entirely to his care, hesitated not to consent to whatever plan he might think promotive of their ultimate escape. Her heart being full of gratitude, love and confidence, found an easy access. They soon arrived at the rock, he leaped into the water, and she, instructed by him, followed close after. They rose into the cavern, and rested from their fears and fatigue, partaking of some refreshment which he had brought there for himself, little thinking at the time, of the happiness that was in store for him. Early in the morning he returned to Vava'u, to avoid suspicion. But did not fail, in the course of the day, to repair again to the place which held all that was dear to him. He brought her mats to lie on; the finest *gnatoo* for a change of dress; the best of food for her support, sandalwood oil, cocoa nuts, and everything he could think of to render her life as comfortable as possible. He gave her as much of his company as prudence would allow, and at the most appropriate times, lest the prying eye of curiosity should find out his retreat. He pleaded his tale of love with the most impassioned eloquence, more than sufficient to win her warmest affections, for she owed her life to his prompt and generous exertions, at the risk of his own. And how much was he delighted, when he heard the confession from her own lips, that she had long regarded him with a favourable eye, but a sense of duty had caused her to smother the growing fondness, till the late misfortune of her family, and the circumstances attending her escape, had revived all her latent affections, to bestow them wholly upon a man to whom they were so justly due! How happy were they in this solitary retreat! Tyrannic power now no longer reached them, shut out from the world and all its cares and perplexities; secure from all the eventful changes attending upon greatness, cruelty and ambition, themselves were the only powers they served, and they were infinitely delighted with this simple form of government. But although this asylum was their great security in their happiest moments, they could not always enjoy each other's company; it was equally necessary to their safety that he should often be absent from her, and frequently for a length of time together lest his conduct should be watched. The young chief therefore panted for an opportunity to convey her to happier scenes, where his ardent imagination pictured to him the means of procuring for her every enjoyment and comfort. Nor was it long before, an opportunity offering, he devised the means of restoring her with safety to the cheerful light of day. He signified to his inferior chiefs and matabooles, that it was his intention to go to the Fiji Islands, and he wished them to accompany him with their wives and female attendants, but he desired them on no account to mention to the latter the place of their destination, lest they should inadvertently betray their intention, and the governing chief prevent their departure. A large canoe was soon got ready and every necessary preparation made for the voyage. As they were on the point of departure, they asked him if he would not take a Tonga wife with him. He replied, No! but he should probably find one on the way. This they thought a joke, but in obedience to his orders they said no more, and, everybody being on board, they put out to sea. As they approached the shores of the island, he directed them to steer to a certain point, and having come close to a rock, according to his orders, he got up, and desired them to wait there while he went into the sea to fetch his wife. Without staying to be asked any questions, he sprung into the water from the side of the canoe furtherest from the rock, swam under the canoe, and proceeded forward into the sanctuary which had so well concealed his greatest and dearest treasure. Everybody on board was exceedingly surprised at his strange conduct, and began to think him insane. After a little lapse of time, not seeing him come up, they were greatly alarmed for his safety, imagining a shark must have seized him. Whilst they were all in the utmost concern, debating what was best to be done, whether they ought to dive down after him, or wait according to his orders, for that perhaps he had only swum round and was come up in some niche of the rock, intending to surprise them—their wonder was increased beyond all powers of expression, on seeing him rise to the surface of the water, and come into the canoe with a beautiful female. At first they mistook her for a goddess, and their astonishment was not lessened when they recognised her countenance, and found her to be a person, whom they had no doubt was killed in the general massacre of her family. This they thought must be her apparition; but how agreeably was their wonder softened down into the most interesting feelings, when the young chief related to them the discovery of the cavern and the whole circumstance of her escape! They arrived safe at one of the Fiji Islands and resided with a certain chief during two years; at the end of which time, hearing of the death of the tyrant of Vava'u, the young chief returned there with his wife, and lived long in peace and happiness."

There, in the ornate prose of the early nineteenth century is the story of the great romance of the cave. Did you, while following the stirring adventures of the young couple, note how they entered the cave as easily as you or I might pass through an open door? I pointed those passages out to Farquhar. He was not impressed. "They were Tongans," he said. "They'd been diving all their lives. You're not and you haven't been."

He was perfectly right, but a little later when a young American couple who had stopped in Vava'u in the course of yachting through the Pacific, proposed that we all go down the harbour for a picnic and go into the cave afterwards, I spoke again of my desire to go. Then Farquhar said wearily, "Go if you must and get it out of your system."

"You'll come for the picnic, won't you?" I asked, but he shook his head.

"I can't. I have to prepare my weekly lecture for the hospital staff."

I knew he was glad to disassociate himself from what he considered my folly, but quite aside from his feelings about the cave, he was freeing himself from something he didn't want to do anyway. Never was he a picnic man. The dining-room was, in his mind, the proper place in which to enjoy food, with, perhaps, an occasional buffet supper on the veranda. Not for him the joys of sandy sandwiches, charred meat and salt mistaken for sugar.

So Farquhar was missing from the picnic. Missing, too, when the day came, was picnic weather. When we had planned the trip, the sun had shone brilliantly, but now, on the day itself, it was cloudy and blowy with scuds of rain sweeping across the sky every now and then. I recognised the weather as the miserable sort that sometimes fastens itself so tenaciously over the world that one feels it will never change, but John and Mary, who knew less about South Pacific weather, were more hopeful. "It will blow over," they said and, to cover all eventualities, added, "If it doesn't at least we won't get sunburned."

They had anchored in front of the house and when it became

L

obvious that—the weather notwithstanding, the excursion was on. Farquhar paddled us out to the yacht on his way to the hospital. Tami and Tupou clambered eagerly aboard.

"I wish you were coming, too," I said to him as I started to follow them.

"Go along and enjoy yourself," he replied, "but don't let the girls go into the cave." He gave me his hand to help me up and added, "Take care of yourself."

When I got on board the yacht, I saw somewhat to my surprise that Tongo, one of the 'Utulei men, was on board. Later when I asked John why he had brought him, he reminded me of the talk we had had when we planned the day. "You said it was a good idea to get a man to guide us into the cave."

I had, indeed, said so, but I had been thinking of a strong fellow from one of the islands close to the cave who was used to going into it and taking people in—one who might drag me in on a knotted rope. Tongo, the laziest of all our village men, was a notorious "yacht chaser". Whenever a new one sailed into the harbour, he took his disarming smile and his store of old Tongan stories and, hoping to exchange them for clothes, food, small tools, and whatever else was being handed out, climbed aboard. Judging by the layer of blubber-like fat which padded him, he must have prospered in his work, but as a guide to the cave, he inspired me with something less than confidence. "He volunteered," John said and, as Tongo was there, and we had already sailed past the end of our island, I contented myself with saying, "Oh."

The trip down the harbour is always beautiful, but the beauty that day was, for the most part, hidden behind clouds which, after a while, opened up and deluged us with their contents so that we all retreated to the cabin below. About the size of an ordinary dining-room table, it was a jumble of books, plates, clothes and miscellaneous yachting gear. We squeezed into the lower bunks and watched the sea rising and falling through the port holes until Tupou moaned and bolted up the ladder. When she came back, she was grey as the sea. For the rest of the trip, she lay stretched out on an upper bunk vowing eternal hatred for all boats and for everything connected with the sea. Tami was scarcely happier. The thin sweater she had worn was so woefully inadequate that soon she started to shiver. Mary wrapped her in a thick blanket. She and John put on windbreakers. I was cosy enough in my old blue sweatshirt, but we were not at all the sort of picnic-going crowd you see pictured on South Sea island travel folders.

"Let's go down to the cave first," Mary suggested. "Maybe by the time we've been in and out of there, the weather will have improved and we'll feel more like a picnic." John and Tami and I agreed. Tupou said it made no difference to her what we did for she never wanted to eat again.

We sailed on glumly until, through the rainsplashed porthole, we saw a dark grey mass of rocky cliff.

"Is that it?" John called down from the cockpit where he was steering. Tongo stirred out of his snooze and peered out.

"That's it," he said, and he lumbered out of the cabin and up onto the deck. Mary, Tami and I followed and watched while he pointed out the approximate location of the cave entrance. "Go on, go on," he urged John. "Get closer so we can dive off the boat."

But John said, "I can't take the boat any closer. We'd be dashed against the rocks."

"We're too close now," he shouted suddenly as a massive wave swept us so near that we could see the jagged points on the face of the cliff. Closer and closer we came, until it seemed that we must certainly crash against the side of the island, but John was a good seaman. There was a sickening lurch as we heeled over. The yacht straightened and we were speeding away from the island. When we were the distance of a long city block from it, he turned off the engine. It had begun to rain again. Mary, Tami and I went down below while Tongo helped John put down the anchor.

"Aren't we going to stop?" Tupou asked, raising her head weakly from the pillow.

"We have stopped," Mary told her, but Tupou was not convinced . . . and no wonder! Each wave that came crashing against the side of the yacht made her lean over until it seemed she would lie on her side in the sea. Then a cross-current would carry her up and she would tug at the anchor with a wild churning motion.

"Oi-au-e!" Tupou moaned, reverting in her agony to the traditional wail of her people. "Oi-au-e! Why did I ever come?"

In strict contrast to Tupou's misery, John came dripping into the cabin singing out with a gaiety that was obviously meant to restore our spirits. "Here we are at Nuapapu. Bathing suits everybody and we'll be off to Mariner's cave."

"The girls can't go," I said and Tami's strong voice and Tupou's weak one replied together, " Who'd want to?"

Mary was the next drop-out. "I'll stay with the girls," she said. " I'm not that good a swimmer. I'd never make it."

I was beginning to feel that Mary was wise. " That leaves only Tongo and you and me," I said to John, hoping he would decide to call the whole thing off, but he was undaunted by weather or waves.

"Let's go," he said.

In a few minutes the three of us were up on deck bracing ourselves against the wind. Tongo pointed to the cliff before us. " Look there," he said, " see the rock sitting out from the cliff, like a little shelf, close to the water."

John squinted through the rain, saying at last, " I see it—a very narrow ledge," and he, too, pointed and asked me, " You see it?"

" I guess so," I said, straining my near-sighted eyes.

" Swim there and rest a bit before you go into the cave," Tongo said. " The entrance is just beside it."

" Right," said John as he dived into the waves. Tongo shivered and muttered something under his breath about mad *papalangis*, but he, too, went into the sea, flopping like a great awkward fish. I looked down at the angry water and turned to grasp the rail, but this was what I had been talking about for years. Finally I had gained—if not Farquhar's approval, at least his grudging consent. In I went. Over me swept the grey sea waves, like waves of fear through which I struggled choking and sputtering to the surface. I had been swimming for what seemed a very long time, when I stopped, caught my breath and looked about. I could see neither John nor Tongo but the sheer rock wall with its narrow shelf was visible far ahead. Somewhere behind me was the yacht, but it was lost in a swell. The narrow shelf ahead was the only certainty in all the wet spume-filled world, so I made for it. Up a dull glassy mountain I swam, then an abrupt plunge down and up again in a never ending monotony until finally my flailing hand touched rock and John and Tongo were on the ledge above me stretching out helping hands. When they had pulled me up beside them, the three of us stood there shivering and forlorn. Over what seemed miles of sea, the yacht was visible bobbing up and down through a foggy raincloud, but we could not make out any people. " I guess Mary and Tami are down below with Tupou," John said. " No audience, so we may as well go. Where's the entrance?"

Tongo pointed straight ahead. " There," he said and then, shifting his finger to the left, " No, there, I guess." I followed his wavering hand, but I saw no dancing blue circle on the dull grey surface. As far as I could see, the sea was the same dead colour. As I stared at it, my determination ebbed away from me. To plunge into a shining circle of light is one thing, but to go into a grey sea beating against a rock wall is quite another. Ruefully and somewhat illogically I thought, " if I kill myself, Farquhar will be angry." My cowardly thoughts were interrupted by John's cheery voice. " Go on," he said to Tongo. " I'll follow you," but Tongo shook his head. " You first."

" Do you want to come with me?"

I lowered my head and acknowledged defeat. " No, John. I'm afraid. I can't see a thing."

John was kind. " It's really rough," he said. " Why don't you just swim back to the yacht?"

" And you?" I asked, hoping for company.

He was made of sterner stuff. " I'll try to get in," he said and flung himself into the water. It closed at once over his head and there was only a thin trail of bubbles to show where he had been.

" Go on," I said to Tongo, but he slunk cravenly back against the wall.

" No, I cannot go into the cave today."

" Then you'll come back to the boat with me?" I asked feeling that even Tongo would be better than the empty sea on my own.

" I'll wait for John," he said and in his tone and in his pale face, I saw the reflection of my own fear.

" Stay if you like, but I'll go now." I slid off the shelf into the water and started swimming. The least I could do, I told myself bitterly, was to get back to the yacht before John came out of the cave, so I went on until my breath grew short and my right leg went limp with cramp. I foundered then, but Mary's voice came encouragingly across the waves. " Just a little bit more," she called and then, " Here, give me your hand."

In another minute, she had helped me up and I staggered wearily into the cabin. Tupou lifted her head and Tami peered out from the depths of her blanket. " Did you get in?" they asked. I had to admit that I had not made it.

"At least you tried," Mary said, wanting to soften my defeat.

I got dressed and we sat for awhile in the rolling cabin until she grew worried about John. "Let's go back up on deck and see if there's any sign of him," she suggested.

When we got up, we could see him standing on the ledge talking to Tongo. "I wonder what's the matter?" Mary said. "They seem to be arguing."

As she spoke John dived into the sea and swam towards us. In what seemed a remarkably short time, he was climbing up the rope ladder. "Did you get in?" we chorused.

"Yes," he said. "It was wonderful. I'll tell you about it, but first I have to go and get Tongo."

"Get Tongo?"

"Yes," he said angrily. He turned to me. "I know you thought Tongo was not the ideal guide and you were right. Not only would he not go into the cave, but now he's afraid to leave the rock. He says he can't possibly swim back to the yacht. I'll have to get the dinghy down and go for him."

"It's not safe," Mary objected. "You'll smash the dinghy and yourself on those rocks."

John shrugged his shoulders. "What can I do? I can't leave him there." So get the dinghy he did and we stood on deck watching him go—a bright white spot on the sea, bobbing up and down like a cork. A real seaman, John seemed to be able to calculate instinctively the surge of the waves as he let them carry him close to the ledge and hold to it just long enough for Tongo to flop into the dinghy. Another surge and a great rush and they were off, sliding back toward us on a receding wave. Tongo sat, a dejected figure, while John pulled on the oars and brought the dinghy smartly up against the yacht. Tongo roused from his apathy long enough to scramble on board and to catch the painter and hold it until John followed him up. When the dinghy had been brought up and made fast, it began to rain again and we all went down below. A picnic on shore was out of the question so Mary brought out the sandwiches and we munched on them as we sailed dejectedly up the harbour.

That night when I confessed my defeat to Farquhar, I said, "I'll wait now until the girls are grown up and through school," but I knew even as I said the words, and he knew, too, that my defeat was final. Only in my imagination shall I ever see that cave.

So much for my defeat. Now to Byron's. He never saw the cave, either. In fact, he never even saw the entrance—neither blue and sparkling on a sunny day, nor obscured in the general greyness of a dull one. Somewhere in Europe, he ran across the French edition of Mariner's Tonga and his imagination brought him as close as he ever came to these shores. Had he been satisfied to put Mariner's story of the lovers into verse, he might have written a masterpiece. Unfortunately he read another story of Tonga—Bligh's account of the famous mutiny on the Bounty which took place off the island of Tofua in the Ha'apai group, south of Vava'u. He stirred the two tales into an unlikely mixture, fitted the Tongan maiden with an imaginary white mutineer lover from the Hebrides—Torquil, " son of northern seas " and produced an atrocity called " The Island " which, although it fills out a few pages in his collected works, does nothing to further his reputation. Whenever I read his account of the amorous housekeeping that his Neuha and Torquil set up in the cave, I laugh, remembering what John told us on the day of my defeat. The beautiful mist does, of course, keep the place in a state of perpetual dampness and the surge which causes it alters the air pressure so that ones ears pop constantly. But Byron, no doubt, would have said that love conquers all—even a sopping bed and popping ears.

CHAPTER TWENTY-FIVE

A CASE HISTORY

GENERALLY SPEAKING medical case histories make pretty dull reading, but one there was that was as full of excitement as an adventure story and that had a surprise ending as good as any O. Henry ever dreamed up.

For several years Farquhar worked with a group of doctors who, stationed all over the Pacific, were studying the important subject of fish poisoning. The Case of the Eel he wrote up in the sort of scientific shorthand acceptable in professional circles, but when he and the MO's spoke of it, it became a tragic saga.

It began one dark rough night when a group of men from Tu'unuku village went out fishing. At first they rowed up and down in the harbour near the village, but their luck was very bad. They caught nothing but one little fish that was scarcely big enough to cut up for bait.

" We must go further out," said one of the men, " out beyond the end of the island to the deep open sea."

" It is too rough," someone murmured, but the voices of the other men rose against the timid one.

What did the darkness or the wind matter to them? They knew the waters around the islands as well as they knew their own homes. What was a rough sea to strong men? Their families expected them to come home with fish for a good meal and they were not going to disappoint them.

Resolutely they turned and rowed toward the end of the main island and beyond it into the turbulent open sea. Not until the thunder of waves crashing against the sheer rocky sides of Tu'unga Sika, the guardian islet, was only a muted roar did they stop and throw their lines into the sea.

An hour passed and two and they had not had one bite. " Let's go home," the timid one said. " If it's to be a hungry night, we'd be better in our own warm beds."

But the others would not go home empty handed, although the seas had risen so that their boat rocked madly in the darkness and they were all soaked from spray.

It was midnight when the first man felt a tug at his line. Excitedly, he pulled it in. There was nothing on it, but he was not discouraged. " The bait's gone. Now we know there are fish about," he said cheerfully.

Then one line after another jerked and was pulled up and from every one, the bait was gone. At last only one line remained, the heaviest of them all. Suddenly, it pulled taut and the man who held it cried out to his companions. " It's a big one. I've got it this time."

Then he cried out again, " Help me. I can't hold it alone."

Those standing nearest to him grabbed onto the line and together hand over hand they pulled.

The timid one fumbled in his basket for his torch and flashed its dim light onto the black waters just in time to see their surface broken by the convulsive flailings of a long sinuous body.

" It's an eel," he shouted, " a tremendous eel," and he kept the light on as the men pulled. At last the creature's head with its evil unlidded eyes and its cruel mouth snapped viciously over the hook, appeared over the side of the boat.

Then began a great struggle as the men tried to pull all the long body into the boat. As big around as the strongest man's thigh it was and so slippery that a man no sooner grasped it than it slipped from his arms and plopped back into the sea. But those who held the line stood firm and one found his bush knife and slashed at the wicked head. Wildly the creature fought against the men and against death, but death and men prevailed at last. Covered with blood and exhausted, they fell back and lay panting against the still convulsive coils of the eel.

The timid one huddled down in the bow of the boat pushed the trembling body away and shuddered. " Let us go home now," he begged. The others would gladly have done as he wished, but in the struggle, the strength had gone out of them—even out of the strongest one. " We must rest awhile," they said. " Then we will go home," and they fell into a coma-like sleep against the cold body of the eel.

When they awoke, they were far out at sea, but, undaunted, they began at once to row. The dark sky had grayed by the time they passed Tu'unga Sika and long before they reached their village, the sun was high in the sky.

As they came within sight of the beach, they saw that some of the women and children were walking along the shore.

"They thought we were lost," said the timid one, but the others gave a great shout. "Food for everyone," they cried. "Come and help us carry it in."

They leaped triumphantly from the boat as soon as it was beached and, pulling the great eel out, carried it up to the village and stretched it on a grassy place where everyone could see it.

Ten feet long it was—and more, and the old men marvelled at it, saying, "It must have come from the distant volcanic islands. There was never one so big caught here."

The children prodded its skin with their fingers, feeling beneath the slime to the odd rectangular scales. The girls exclaimed at its ugliness, but the women who tended the fires said, "Cut it up quickly. We will put it in the pots and boil it; for we are all hungry."

It must have been almost noon when the meat was cooked and pots of big white yam to go with it. Thirty grown people and as many children as could crowd in sat down to eat.

"There were twenty-five of them in the hospital," Farquhar reported when he came home the next day. "Half of them we treated and sent back to the village, but the others are still in."

On the following day, he told of the death of six dogs and four pigs that had eaten the remains of the eel.

"And the people?" I asked.

"The ones in the hospital are still terribly sick," he said, "but I think they'll do—all except two. They ate large quantities of the meat and then they drank the juice the eel had been boiled in."

Ma'afu, one of the doctors at the hospital, had the theory that the eel—so much larger than any ever found in the harbour, must have come in from the distant chain of volcanic islands that parallels the Vava'u group.

"I think he's right," Farquhar said. "From reports coming in from all over the Pacific, its seems there are more cases of poisoning recorded from volcanic islands than from anywhere else."

The following day one of the men on the critical list died. "We did everything we could to save him," said Farquhar, "but he never had a chance."

That afternoon when I typed up his case notes, I thought few deaths could be more unpleasant. Violent vomiting, convulsions, weakening heart action, a rally, and then the whole thing over again and again until at last the heart froze in paralysis and gave out.

"What about the others?" I asked.

"They've all gone home feeling pretty sorry for themselves but they'll be all right—all except the other man who drank the juice."

Long before then I had learned that—although doctors try to keep their work on a purely scientific level, there is no such thing as the impersonal practice of medicine. As the days passed, I knew what anxiety Farquhar felt for the patient who still remained in the hospital. Once, referring to the notes I had typed, I asked, "Is he still so sick?" and Farquhar replied grimly. "Yes, it's hell for him. He must have a terrific constitution to be able to stand it so long."

And then, one day about a week after the fateful meal, Farquhar came home smiling so broadly that I knew it was safe to ask about his patient.

"Yes," he said. "He's out of danger."

"How lucky he was you were there," I said, but Farquhar only laughed.

"It's true that he was saved by medical science," he said. "It's even true I did it—but I did it long ago, not this week."

"Long ago?" I echoed, not understanding.

Then he explained that some four years ago, the man had been brought into hospital suffering from intestinal adhesions and obstructions. "I had to remove about eight feet of his intestines," he said, "And that's what's saved his life now."

"How?"

"Well," Farquhar explained, "Because of the missing eight feet of intestines, he had that much less chance to absorb the poison into his body and so he escaped the death which overtook the other man who had a normal lot of intestines."

Even from the medical notes, there emerges a feeling of triumph at the surprise escape of the man with the shortened intestines and a sense of horror at an eel big enough to feed—and poison thirty people.

CHAPTER TWENTY-SIX

A TONGAN TRIANGLE

INCONSISTENCY IS, I often think, man's dominant trait. All the outside world talks of peace and wages war. When, in the last century, Tongans became Christians, they thought, with more logic than other nations display, that war was incompatible with the teachings of Jesus, and so abandoned it. But Tongans, too, talk of peace. In its purely local context it applies to those personal relationships which enable men to live together in harmony. Tongans talk of peace, but they are as inconsistent as other men and sometimes, when they find it, reject it, as they rejected the household of Leni who lived in a nearby village.

Originally Leni was a Nuku'alofa school teacher. He had not gone to the Government Training College, nor even passed his lower leaving examination; so, how he happened to get into the profession, I do not know. Probably, like many young Tongans with white-collar instincts, he had developed a dislike for bush work and decided that sitting in a shady school room dozing through the warm days while the village youngsters chattered about him, was a more suitable occupation for one of his talents. Perhaps he got the job in the first place by making a picnic for some former Director of Education or by giving a few well chosen presents to the local School Inspector. At any rate, he might have ended his days as a teacher had it not been that just as he was rounding into plump middle age, a new Director of Education was appointed. The new man was an energetic New Zealander who had two revolutionary ideas about teachers. First, he believed they should be trained, and, second, he felt it imperative that, having been trained, they should teach. His notions caused a terrible upset in the education department and created endless confusion in the lives of innumerable teachers including that of Leni who presently found himself deprived of his school and of the salary which had enabled him to keep himself in neat white shirts and *valas*.

Leni, however, was more resourceful than the Director suspected. As he had not the slightest intention of working in the bush, he began at once to think how he might go on living the same sort of pleasant life to which he had become accustomed. As a first step, he decided that he needed a fresh perspective on life. As nothing is so quickly productive of that as a change of scene, he got on the *Aoniu* and sailed for Vava'u. Here he had a remote cousin. In Tongan terms that is to say, here he had a hotel. In typical Polynesian manner, he entered his relative's house, set down his bed roll and his basket and announced that he had come for a visit. He was fed, his clothes were washed, and he was supplied with a bit of pocket money. Beyond that, he was very little trouble to his cousin. He used his house merely as a base from which each morning, as soon as he had had his breakfast, he set out to seek his fortune. He did that—not in the common *papalangi* way of trying to get a job at one of the stores, nor yet in the usual Tongan way of going to help his cousin work in the bush garden, but in his own way of pacing up and down the streets of Neiafu.

One day while he was thus engaged in walking about town, he came to big old timber house surrounded by a well tended garden. He stopped to admire it and when he saw a passer-by, asked him who lived there. He was told that an old widow called Mele lived there all alone.

" All alone?" He asked.

" Yes," replied his informant. " She had only one child—a daughter. She's married and lives down in Tonga, so Mele's alone except for a few boys and girls who stay there and help her about the place and work in her bush land."

" Ah," said Leni. " She has bush land, too?"

" Yes, indeed, a very good bush in the fertile place out near Leimatu'a."

Leni thanked the man for his information and went back to his cousin's house to have a nap. The next day he did not have to think twice which direction to take. Directly to the old widow's house he went and stood in the road before it.

After a time, a little bird-like woman with close-cropped white hair came round the corner of the house and, seeing him standing looking into her garden asked, " Do you want something?"

For just a second, looking at her rough, work-stained hands, Leni paused, then he smiled and said, " Well, as a matter of fact, I do want something. I'm looking for a wife."

The widow Mele squinted up her eyes and looked critically at him. " That should be easy for a fine fat fellow like you," she said pleasantly. " This village is full of eager young girls."

Leni shrugged his shoulders. " That's just the trouble," he said slowly. " These Vava'u girls are always after me, but—well, I prefer a woman a little older . . . one who's lived a bit and learned how to take care of a man."

Mele looked down at her bare brown feet with their wrinkled skin and the toes with broken nails and reflected that she must have been fifteen years old, maybe more, the year Leni had been born, but when she looked up again, he was still smiling and what was more, he had in his eyes the sort of provocative glint she had never expected to see again.

Unconsciously she smoothed the faded dress over her scrawny hips. " I've lived some," she admitted and taking up all her courage added, " A fine young man like you would be a joy to take care of."

In Tonga some things happen very quickly. A visit to the court house, a stop at the Wesleyan church, a shopping tour to buy a tin of corned beef to make *lu pulu*, and two lives are changed forever.

So it was with Leni and Mele. For awhile after the wedding whenever Leni appeared at the kava circles there were pointed allusions to people who married—not a woman, but a house and a bush land, but Leni smiled and drank his kava and gave no sign that he heard. At *tapa*-making parties, the women openly admired Mele's new husband. " He's so nice and fat," they said.

One woman frowned. " He's a bit small," but " Hush," the others cried. " The small ones are very often the best of all."

As for Mele, she blushed like a girl, covered her face with her hands and giggled.

And then time passed and the village won a football game, the stores ran out of flour, the Queen went to England—and with all the fresh news, Leni and Mele dropped into the obscurity of the usual.

The conventional idea of the husband as provider did not appeal to Leni, but he was so polite and so pleasant that Mele was only too glad to go off to the bush with the girls and boys, to dig up yams and carry them back home to cook for him. She was a good weaver, too, and she managed to sell enough baskets to the tourists to provide all the cash they needed—enough to buy Leni's white shirts and *valas*, enough to buy the soap to wash them and the starch to make them stiff and shiny—enough, too, to keep him in the cigarettes he loved to smoke as he walked about town—enough, indeed, so that he cast no lingering longing glances back to the old days of teaching.

A cynical person might feel that Leni contributed little to the household, but something, certainly, he gave it. Mele's old eyes sparkled with fresh delight and her dry lips were always curved in a smile. Anyone coming on her unexpectedly invariably caught her singing some old song.

Misfortune, though, comes to the happiest of mortals. One wet day, coming home from planting kumalas in the bush, Mele caught a cold. She had had colds before and thought nothing of it although she shivered through her bath and shook as she set about preparing Leni's dinner. When it was cooked and she had served him, she had no interest in eating her own share, but, instead, lay down on her mat. She could not get up again and that night the girls that stayed with them cleaned up. They were well-trained and the next day she was able to direct them so that Leni was taken care of almost as well as if she had done it herself. However, when several days had gone by and Mele was no better, Leni began to think. At the end of the week, he said to her, "Mele, we are getting old, you and I. We need a young man to take care of the bush for us. There's plenty of room in this house . . ."

The result of the conversation was that in a very short time Leni's brother, Seto, arrived from Nuku'alofa. He was a younger man than Leni and a bigger one, but in many ways he resembled him. He liked, for instance, to be taken care of and work was very little to his taste. Fortunately, not long after he arrived, Mele's wiry good health returned and she was strong enough to take care of both men.

It was Leni's habit, after he had eaten in the morning, to dress himself carefully, get a bit of cigarette money from Mele and saunter into town. There he leaned against the wall of the post-office veranda or sat on the bench in front of the kiosk and talked to his friends. Seto fell very easily into his brother's habits. One day as they went into town Leni asked, "What do you think of my wife?"

"Not much," Seto said frankly. "She's too old for my taste." Leni chuckled. "Take a look at the house and the bush land. You'll think better of her."

So Seto looked at the house and the bush. It did not make him change his opinion of his sister-in-law, but it did make him feel that he could be quite content living with Mele and Leni forever.

Nevertheless, things were not fated to go on as they had been doing. One Saturday morning at market, Seto saw a fine fat woman selling spring onions. He bought a whole armful of them and took them home to Mele to put in the stew. The next week he visited the market again and bought another armful of onions. He discovered that the fair seller came from an island down the harbour and that her name was Tuli. Having learned those things, Seto wandered away from his brother's house, but in a few weeks he wrote to invite Leni and Mele to his wedding. He would, he said, be married in Neiafu so that he could be married in the big church by the head minister and so, too, that he and Tuli could spend their honeymoon with his dear brother and sister-in-law.

To Leni and Mele, Seto's plans seemed perfectly natural. Here in Tonga all the most proper honeymoons are spent with a host of accompanying relatives—the more there are, the more prestige the new couple enjoys.

Happily, Mele scrubbed the house and prepared new mats and tapa for the marriage bed. In due time, the wedding took place and Seto and Tuli moved in. The honeymoon stretched from weeks to months and still they stayed, but why should they not? The welcome was as fresh as ever. Mele and Leni had grown used to Seto before the wedding and they both found Tuli a delight. If it was true that she had more than a girlish share of plumpness, it was also true that her sleek black hair was still glossy and her olive flesh was firm and clean and perfumed with Tongan oil. Her eyes were round and full and had a quality Victorian novelists used to describe as "melting". She was clever about the house, too, and could weave as well as Mele could. From the beginning the two women were friends who spoke freely of their love for one another. Leni loved Tuli, too. He loved her more and more as time went on . . .

Until at last, Seto objected to his love and the brothers fell to quarrelling. All too late, Seto realised that the heart of his bride had been stolen from him—stolen twice over for both Leni and

Mele loved her and she loved both of them. Suddenly the house—big though it was, became too small for the four people who lived in it. For a while it was crowded with bickering, bad temper and unhappiness, but all that ended one day when the *Aoniu* came in. Seto said nothing to anyone, but he bought himself a ticket back to Nuku'alofa and that night when the *Aoniu* sailed, he sailed on her, renouncing as he did so, his beautiful Tuli and his easy life in Vava'u.

The deserted wife stayed with Mele and Leni. Nothing was more natural. Nothing could have been happier, either. The three of them enjoyed one another so much that they scarcely noticed that Seto had gone. To the neighbours, too, the arrangement seemed ideal until they noticed that Leni shared Tuli's sleeping mat more often than he did Mele's. Then the gossip started.

Surely the three of them must have heard the neighbours whispering, but they never gave any sign that they did ... nor did they alter in any least way their mode of life. An observer from another planet, coming first on the threesome and noting their tender consideration for one another and the harmony that filled their lives, might well have concluded that all Tongan households are triangular affairs. They are not. From the fact that they are not stemmed the only unhappiness that ever clouded the lives of Leni and the two women whom the neighbours had already begun to refer to as his two wives. As Mele and Tuli were both Vava'u women, they had many relatives living nearby. Not one of the relatives approved of them. Mele's only child by her first marriage, a daughter, came up from Tonga to visit every now and then. Whenever she was in the house, she grumbled mightily, calling Tuli "harlot" and "whore" and all sorts of other uncomplimentary names which she said she found in her well-thumbed Bible. As her own children grew older, she sent them to Vava'u to remonstrate with their grandmother on her evil life.

But neither family disapproval nor neighbourhood gossip was strong enough to upset the happiness of the strange household, nor was poverty, which came to them after a time. Mele still had her bush land, but as her family grew increasingly more annoyed at her for cherishing both Leni and Tuli, the supply of grandsons, nephews and more remote relatives who had lived with her and worked the bush for her, dwindled and finally stopped.

There were those who thought Leni might have gone to work

in the bush himself, but neither of his wives urged him to do so. To both Mele and Tuli, it was a matter of pride that Leni's hands were soft and smooth, unstained by working in the soil. It was a joy they shared—seeing him go off to town each morning, resplendent in white *vala* and shirt. And when he had gone, they sang as they trudged off together to dig the yams for his dinner.

There came some bad years when their bush lands failed to feed them. Then Mele and Tuli gladly became beggars for the sake of the man they loved. Every morning as soon as the neighbours lit their morning fires, one of them would go visiting. Sometimes it was Tuli who bravely went into a nearby house and asked if they could give her a bit of food in exchange for some work. Sometimes Mele shuffled disconsolately into a strange dining-room and sat looking hungry until the kindly people fed her. Technically, they were not beggars because in Tonga no one ever has to ask for food. He has only to appear in a house at meal time to have a place set for him. Generous though they are, Tongans are only human. Although they willingly fed Mele and Tuli whenever they appeared they laughed over the way the two women always came with a little basket into which they would put the greater part of whatever was given them to eat. Some of the young people would tease Mele until she would confess, " It's for poor Leni." Tuli would cry discreetly, " It's for my household," and the young ones would nudge one another and giggle. Soon, however, the neighbours grew used to them and would even set aside a little basket of food to await their coming. Leni himself never stooped to visiting the neighbours at mealtime. Why should he, when he had two such loving wives to collect for him?

And so the years passed. When news was scarce, people gossiped about the threesome, but for the most part, they simply accepted them. As time went on, Mele grew thinner and more stooped, Tuli's black hair was laced with white and she grew heavier and slower in her movements. Only Leni, plump pleasant little man that he was, seemed unchanging . . . and unchanging, too, was the love which held the three of them together.

Tuli grew older and Mele grew frailer, but it was Leni, the sheltered and cared for one that time touched so lightly, who died first. A particularly virulent sort of flu swept through the country one year and before the two wives had time to realise what had happened, they were widows.

Happy in life, Leni was blessed in death. Where ordinary men have one loving heart to mourn them, he had two. Both Mele and Tuli donned funeral mats, both tore their hair and hacked it off as widows should and both pierced the air with the sharp "*Oiaue, Oi-au-e*" of wailing.

When the minister had spoken the last words over Leni, his widows sat in the mute companionship of grief and oiled the smooth black pebbles that ornamented his grave and when, at last, they had performed their final duties to their husband, they went home together to pick up the remains of their life. In such sad and loving unity they might have gone on until death had claimed them in their turn, but the world that talks of peace and will not allow it when it exists, pushed its way between them.

Mele's righteous daughter decided that she simply must make a decent woman of her mother. She came to Vava'u one day when Mele was out of the house and suddenly began shouting and swearing at Tuli. Her two hefty sons joined her and together they drove the poor widow into the street. Throwing her sleeping mat and a basket containing all her clothes after her, they threatened to take her to court if she ever returned.

When Mele came home, she called to Tuli, but there was no Tuli to answer. In her place was Mele's unfeeling daughter who said, "That evil woman has gone . . . and may she go and eat her grandfather."

When poor old Mele understood what had happened, she tried to run out of the house and search for Tuli, but her daughter pushed her roughly away from the door and forced her down onto a mat. All that night the irate daughter paced back and forth pouring out on her mother's bent white head an interminable moral lecture.

The following week, Mele died. The doctor said she had succumbed to the same virus that had carried Leni off. Her daughter said she had died of shame. Tuli sitting in a strange house pondered on the inconsistencies of people who spurn the peace they pretend to seek and mourned red-eyed and silent for her beloved two.

CHAPTER TWENTY-SEVEN

DOCTOR AND FRIEND

Happy years have a way of slipping by that makes those who live them forget time and the changes that time brings. Here in 'Utulei, Farquhar and the girls and I—with Tu'ifua on weekends and special occasions—were busy with our work, our garden, our books and our friends. Now and then we measured the girls on the veranda posts where we marked their height and exclaimed on how tall they had grown. Sometimes when we walked in the garden, Farquhar would point to the big flamboyant tree that spreads its shade over all the lower right side of the garden and laughingly ask, " Do you remember how once you cried when a storm knocked down so much of that tree you were afraid it would never survive?"

" Yes," I would answer, staring up at the thick branches along which Polito walks so easily to tie on the epiphytic ferns and orchids that grow up there. " Yes . . . and I remember planting the seed from which it grew while I was still at the college and carrying the seedling across the harbour in a can when first I came to live here."

In the house, we searched for new spots in which to build book shelves to house our ever-growing library and watched our *tapa*-bound guest book fill with the names of people who came to our dinners or the girls' birthday feasts, of old friends who stayed a month or two and new ones who came to the house for the first time.

Only in such quiet ways did the years give notice that they were passing. Twelve times the seasons turned while we worked and played, recovered from colds and sunburn, kept Christmas, read new books and old, worried about patients and homework, painted the house and poked about the reef looking for sea shells.

Every day brought its own fullness and we had plans and dreams enough for a dozen futures, but suddenly the even pattern of our days was broken.

One morning, Farquhar got up as usual and showered and dressed for the hospital and I went into the garden to get fresh flowers for the house. He was sitting in the living-room when I came in with a big bunch of double pink hibiscus. I stopped to show them to him, but he did not look up nor did he reply to the remark I made. Thinking he had not heard, I spoke again. Then, in a strange broken voice, he said, " Help me! The room is whirling around."

I ran to him and sitting on the arm of his chair, held him firmly against me.

" I was afraid of falling," he whispered. I tightened my arms around him and soon he spoke again, his voice faint, but calm and detached as if he were discussing an old case history. " I've had a stroke," he said.

Because to write is to live again, it has been a joy to chronicle the long years when our lives—like all the green world around us—seemed to begin anew each day. I have tried to write also, of the last six years Farquhar and I had together, but I cannot.

Certainly I can put down the words—three strokes, a gall-stone operation, uremic poisoning, lung cancer—but I cannot record the pain Farquhar suffered nor the agony we knew in watching him suffer. To live once through such a time is enough and more than enough.

And yet, there were things to be thankful for and to remember gladly even in those hard years. Chief among them was the fact that—in spite of the disasters which overtook Farquhar's body, his mind and his spirit remained robust as always so that *he* was always with us. We were grateful, too, that our families and our friends proved to be the durable sort that stood by us in time of trouble. Tevita Puloka, who was in charge of the hospital when Farquhar first became sick and Bill Tufu'i, who replaced him after a year or so, were the best of doctors and the best of friends. But there comes a time when no doctor—however skilful, can help. That time came for Farquhar one afternoon in the hospital in Neiafu where he had spent so many busy happy days at work.

At sunset, we brought him home to 'Utulei for the last time. On the beach to greet us were the villagers. They had no words, but more meaningful were the tears that misted their eyes and the silent embraces they gave to me and to the girls.

Now he lies high on the hill in the village cemetery. From his grave can be seen the wide sweep of sea and islands that he used to say was—but for the coconut trees, so much like his native Scotland. At his head we have put a great round of coral. The plaque on it describes his life here. It says, I think, all he would have wanted it to say. " Farquhar Matheson, Doctor and Friend to the Tongan People."

CHAPTER TWENTY-EIGHT

A CIRCULAR STORY

For all of us, 'Utulei Beach School had been a wonderful experience, but during the last two years of Farquhar's life, it had proceeded with difficulty. There was scarcely a week without some fresh emergency in his physical condition that made it necessary for me to drop everything and try to make him as comfortable as possible here while the girls got the engine into the boat and hurried across the harbour to Neiafu and up to the hospital to find Bill to come across to him.

In time so broken and so filled with anxiety, school slowed and often came to a complete halt. Unfortunately for the academic programme, the deterioration in Farquhar's health came just when they were commencing their high-school work and needed more than ever plenty of uninterrupted time in which to acquire new study techniques. However, quite aside from that, 'Utulei Beach School had run into serious difficulties. A year and more before he died, Farquhar and I had discussed them. In mathematics and in those subjects which depended largely on reading such as English, history and geography, we had been able to give the girls a fine background and—thanks to records and to regular conversation classes with the Sisters, their French was really good, but there remained great gaps in their education. With no laboratory facilities, we had been unable to give them any adequate science courses.

As important as that academic lack was 'Utulei Beach School's inability to offer them a well-rounded social life. When they were in the beginning grades, they played happily every afternoon with the village children. However, by the time they reached high school those local children who were continuing their own education had either gone away to one of the high schools in Nuku'-

alofa or had become boarders at the Wesleyan College in Neiafu. Had any of those schools been up to standard, we would have sent the girls to them, but, in spite of considerable up-grading in recent years, none of them provided a proper background for University work. The majority of the village girls—by the time they were fourteen, simply left school and stayed at home helping the family finances by weaving mats and baskets for tourists while they waited for marriage. Tami and Tupou preserved a fondness for those unfortunate girls, but, with every passing day, they had less in common with them. Wanting for our two, broader horizons, we decided that we would send them to America for their last two years of high school. There they would have an opportunity to make up their science requirements and to be part of a normal teen-aged social group. It would also get them broken in to the faster pace of life in an industrial society before they were ready for University work.

Our decision seemed to us both sensible and possible. We could not, when we made it, foresee how difficult it would be to carry out. But the week before Farquhar died, both Australia and New Zealand froze their currencies. As all the money we had, with the exception of my few US war bonds, was in those two countries, I realised at once that sending the girls away to school had become virtually impossible.

And that is the introduction to what I always think of as " our circular story." The beginnings of it go back to the time of the hurricane and the hero of it is Mata'aisi—our village school teacher who during the storm was such a great help to me both in getting people fed and in keeping up their spirits. A good teacher was Mata'aisi, well liked by both his pupils and the grown ups in the village, but he was not content with the profession. He felt, correctly, that it offered him little future. A serious young man with a very genuine concern for his fellows, he had long dreamed of entering the ministry of the Church of England, thinking it would offer him a wider field of action.

In this country the headquarters of everything—government, business, schools and churches is in the capital, Nuku'alofa. Vava'u is separated from it by only 170 sea miles. When the Nuku'alofa people want something—be it money, copra, pigs, or sea shells, they are immediately in contact. When, however, Vava'u people want something, Nuku'alofa does not hear. Letters are not answered, promises are not kept. Vava'u is suddenly so far away that even thinking about it becomes impossible. When Mata'aisi tried to get information about studying for the ministry, he met with the usual Nuku'alofa reaction to Vava'u. Most of his letters remained unanswered. The few replies he got spoke vaguely of quotas already filled and advised him "to write again next year".

Just after the hurricane, he spoke to me of his disappointment. " I suppose I might as well give up," he said. " They haven't even bothered to answer my last three letters."

Suddenly I had an idea. If Nuku'alofa wouldn't answer, why not by-pass it? " Let me write to the Bishop in Fiji," I suggested. " He's a friend of ours and perhaps he'd help."

Mata'aisi brightened at once. " Would you do that?" he asked eagerly.

Lionel Kempthorne, Bishop of Polynesia, was a clergyman straight out of the pages of Trollop. Well-educated and well-read, he was equally well-versed in such typical British concerns as cricket and the ritual of afternoon tea. Although he was small in stature, his snowy white hair, handsome good looks and impeccable manners combined to give him at all times—even when he was careening over a bumpy island road on an unsteady bicycle, a proper episcopal air. He was, moreover, an understanding man and a fair judge of character.

To him I wrote, " I don't know what you want in a minister, but Mata'aisi has a great concern for people and is genuinely interested in helping them." I added an account of the part he had played in our house during the hurricane, the history of his teaching career, a record of his church membership, and an assortment of recommendations from the villagers.

In a surprisingly short time, I received a fat letter from Fiji. After thanking me for bringing Mata'aisi to his attention, Bishop Kempthorne wrote, " I send you a set of entrance examinations for St. John's Theological Seminary here in Suva. If Mata'aisi can pass them, we will welcome him as a student." He asked me to supervise the papers. Because he well knew the educational limitations of islanders, he added, " Please note. There is no time limit on these papers."

Mata'aisi was elated. For a week, he came down to the house every night. As soon as the dining-table had been cleared, he sat down with a lamp and a freshly-filled fountain pen. I gave him an examination paper and went through to the living-room, leaving him to write. Usually we went to bed early, but that week we sat up yawning until midnight while now he stared at his papers in despair, now groaned aloud and then, in a sudden burst of inspiration wrote furiously. When the week was over, all three of us were tired and rather pessimistic, but I bundled the papers up and sent them off to Fiji.

We were surprised and proud when, in due time, we heard that Mata'aisi had not only passed, but had come at the top of all that year's candidates.

Soon he packed his bag and went off to Fiji. Farquhar and I heard from him often when he was in the seminary and once, when he was in his second year, I visited him there. By that time, Bishop Kempthorne had retired and had been succeeded by the energetic Australian, John Volkner.

The sprawling island diocese over which Bishop Volkner ruled was poor in both money and trained men, but he did not intend it to remain so. A great organiser and fund-raiser, the new Bishop travelled constantly all over the British and American world looking for support for the poor churches and schools of Polynesia. Everywhere he found people generous and eager to help.

One night in Massachusetts, at a dinner given him by the local clergy, he sat next to a tall whimsical man, Dr. Charles Buck, Jr., who was Dean of Boston's St. Paul's Cathedral.

After the Bishop had spoken of his beautiful island diocese and of its desperate need for trained men, Dr. Buck turned to him. " It sounds a wonderful place," he said. " I guess I'll come out on my sabbatical."

The remark might have been a chance one, but the Bishop let no opportunity go unheeded. " Come and teach New Testament for me at St. John's," he urged and soon the two men were deep in discussion.

The following year when Dr. Buck got his sabbatical, he packed his suitcase and taking his wife, Betty, went to Fiji. There, at St. John's, he taught a course in New Testament to a group of theology students who came from all the different islands of the Western Pacific. One of them was Mata'aisi.

Although he was keen on his studies and enjoyed his fellow students, Mata'aisi had, as have all Tongans who leave their homeland, many moments of acute homesickness. When he confided his longings to Dr. and Mrs. Buck, the three became fast friends. As the months passed and he told them ever more of his home in Tonga, the Bucks found themselves wanting to see his islands almost as much as he did. By the time the academic year at St. John's had finished, they decided that, instead of heading straight back to Boston, they would first take a trip on the Tongan government vessel, *Aoniu*. From Fiji, it went to Samoa and then to Tonga where it called at both Vava'u and Nuku'alofa.

Mata'aisi wrote telling of his American friends and asking us to meet them when they came to Vava'u. And so it came about that one morning, Farquhar and I sat in a tiny cabin on the *Aoniu* talking to Charles and Betty Buck. At first glance Charles—tall, lanky, with a close cropped crew cut, looked more like a college track man than the Dean of the Church, but he had a clear-cut, sensitive face, eyes that truly saw the things they looked at and a mouth that found laughter easy. Betty who, in order to accompany Charles during his sabbatical, had taken a leave from Boston's Milton Academy where she heads the Primary Department, was small with the quiet, self-effacing good manners of a true New Englander. As capable as Charles and as good humoured, she had a personality and a will of her own.

The Church of England here in Vava'u is so small that it does not have a resident minister. Services are conducted by a lay reader, but whenever a minister comes by, the congregation seizes on the opportunity to hold a regular service. We knew that they had scheduled a morning service which Charles was to conduct. Indeed, as we talked in the cabin, Tavake, the lay reader, hovered in the passageway, poking his head in every now and then as if he were afraid we might spirit his minister away.

"We want you to come to 'Utulei," we told the Bucks, "but we know you have to go to church. We'll go home now and come back for you after the service."

Betty, perched up on an upper bunk, looked down at us and laughed. "Charles has to go to church, but I don't. You can have me now."

So we left Charles to Tavake and taking Betty, came home to find the girls waiting on the beach for us. With the sure instincts of the young, Tami and Tupou claimed Betty at once. First they took her on a grand tour of the garden and then, the day being calm and the sea perfectly clear, Tami paddled her across the harbour to look at the wonderful tangle of coral which grows on the reef opposite us.

By the time they came back, Charles had arrived from Neiafu and we all had lunch. When it was over Charles and Betty and Farquhar and I went into the living-room. There we spent the entire afternoon. Sometimes Tami and Tupou came in for a while before they wandered off again to play. Sometimes there were just the four of us talking. We had no need to "get to know one another". We talked as we might have done with friends we had known since childhood—of whatever interested us—of books and music, of islands and men, of religion and education.

Love at first sight cannot be explained, but for a few fortunate individuals it is a wonderful and valid experience. Equally wonderful is instant friendship—and equally inexplicable. It occurred on that Vava'u day between the two Bucks and the four of us.

The relationship commenced that day was destined as are all real friendships to grow and flourish. As the only way it could possibly do so, was by correspondence, by correspondence it was. We were—all of us, busy people, so the letters were not frequent, but when they came, it was always as if Charles and Betty had come back for another visit.

When I had to write and tell them of Farquhar's death, I told them, too, of the plans we had made, he and I, to send the girls away to school and of how, because of the currency freeze, I was finding it impossible to carry out our plans.

By return mail, I had a letter that changed life for us all. Charles wrote words of sympathy and of comfort. Then he turned, as we all must, to the living and wrote about the girls. He said that he and Betty had talked and thought much about them. They felt that after the quiet sheltered life they had led in Tonga, a typical American public high school would be impossible for them. He wrote of St. Anne's, a small high school for girls. Located in Boston, it was run by an order of Episcopalian nuns. It was academically sound and the Sisters were dedicated people who took a personal interest in their students. In such a school, the girls could more easily make the transition from Tonga to the faster-paced life of the United States. If, he said, I could meet half the tuition costs, he could find scholarship funds for the rest. Furthermore, he and Betty offered themselves as the girls' "Boston parents" and their home as the girls' Boston home. He enclosed a catalogue for St. Anne's and finished by saying, " Let me know what you think."

When I had finished reading the letter, I called the girls and gave it to them.

" Can you?" asked Tami soberly when she had read it.

" Can I what?"

" Can you meet half the tuition costs?"

I thought quickly. By selling my war bonds, I could just make it. When she heard my " Yes," she began to read the letter all over again.

Soon the mail between Boston and Vava'u became busy as letters flew back and forth. Our days were filled with thoughts of passports and physical examinations, of what to pack and what to leave behind. By August, everything was in order. The girls and I left Vava'u on the *Tofua* and travelled down to Nuku'alofa. There I put them on a plane for Los Angeles where they spent a month with Tami's grandparents before flying on to Boston, to Charles and Betty and St. Anne's and all the new adventures that lay before them.

My "first nun", Sister Gemma, who was stationed in Vava'u when Farquhar and I were married and when Tami was born, is the most cheerful and most hopeful person I have ever known. She quite simply and literally believes that whatever God does is good. When she heard of the hurricane in Vava'u in 1961, she said, " God must be preparing for some great new things."

A year later when she came to Vava'u to spend a holiday at the local convent, she saw for the first time the fine new two-storey cement building which Sister Annuncia had had the Catholic men build for the convent school.

" Isn't it wonderful," she exclaimed. " You see how God planned it?"

I laughed at her gently in my sceptical way, but I think she may be right after all. Perhaps my circular story is one more proof for her of the mysterious way God works—for,

Because of the hurricane, Mata'aisi was here in our house.
Because he was here, we helped him go to Theology school.
Because he was at St. John's, he met Charles and Betty Buck.
Because he met them, we came to know them.

Because we became friends, Tami and Tupou have an uncle Charles and an Aunt Betty, and a whole new life—
Which might never have been had it not been for the hurricane.

CHAPTER TWENTY-NINE

CHANGES

On 4th June 1970, the independence of the kindom of Tonga was declared by King Taufa Ahau Tupou IV. Before that time—although the country had been ruled by the house of Tupou for over a hundred years, it was bound to Great Britain by a Treaty of Friendship which made it, virtually, a British Protectorate.

Now Tonga has chosen to maintain its ties with Great Britain by joining the Commonwealth. Because of that and because the change over was made peaceably with the consent and guidance of the government in London, many people have felt it was of no importance. Nothing could be further from the truth. Just as growing into adulthood is the most important change in the life of an individual, so is the coming to independent status the most meaningful thing that can happen to a country.

Independence has brought freedom which means wider horizons for the people of these islands. It also means new problems and new responsibilities. How will Tonga respond to the challenge of belonging to the family of nations? No one can forsee the future, nor the changes it may bring, but I am confident that Tupou IV is a king who has the wisdom and the strength to lead his people safely through the years ahead. I believe, further, that the people of Tonga who—in spite of the vagaries of fortune, have always managed to retain a generous, warm-hearted interest in their fellow men, will—as their contacts with other nations spread out in an ever widening circle—become a powerful source of good in the world. They will be able to teach again the old simple truths that the busy industrial nations seem to have forgotton—that men are more important than things; that love is the natural bond between people and that, regardless of age or sex, of colour or religion, or of any of the other thousand differences that divide us, we are all equal in the sight of God.

Changes have come to the Kingdom of Tonga. They have come, too, to the house on the point at 'Utulei. For a while after Farquhar died and the girls went away, I lived alone and had little company, but my village neighbours thought that an odd unnatural way of life. After a time I came to agree with them; for, loneliness lurked behind every door of my empty house and the devils of self-pity ran through the halls. To have tried then to share my days with a stranger would have been difficult after the years of intimate family life. Fortunately, I did not have to do so.

Not long after I first came to these islands my friend, Tupou Ha'afoka, who calls herself my Tongan sister, had a daughter whom she named Petilisi—the Tongan version of my name, Patricia.

To have a child named for me was a special honour and a special delight. I watched her grow from a chubby brown baby who often came to play with Tami and Tupou into a serious school girl. Then she moved away to Nuku'alofa and, although for her, as for us, the years spun round, we kept in contact by means of letters and presents and visits. Now, a beautiful young woman, Petilisi has come back to Vava'u to live with me. It is good to hear her singing through the mornings, to watch her chattering with her friends, to know she is somewhere about.

Tu'ifua comes at weekends, as she has done all through the years. Again the house fills with friends new and old. Again I share the simple events of daily life with my village neighbours.

But three of my important people are no longer here. Tami and Tupou have finished their high school days and, still in Boston, have moved on to the more serious business of University. From them come letters about their studies and the new adventures life is bringing to them. Tu'ifua and Petilisi and I write them of the changes that come to Vava'u—of the new hotel and of the airport that will bring the world so much closer—and of the friends who join us in looking forward to the vacation days when they will be at home.

High on the cemetery hill, the grass around Farquhar's grave is green, but on boat days, his Scotch flag flies as bravely as ever between the red flag of Tonga and the Stars and Stripes. And there are memories enough of the happiness we shared to light all the years to come.